LLC & S-CORPORATION
BEGINNER'S GUIDE
2 BOOKS IN 1

The Most Complete Guide on How to Form,
Manage Your LLC & S-Corp and Save on
Taxes as a Small Business Owner

Steven Carlson

TABLE OF CONTENTS

S-CORP Beginner's Guide (Updated Edition) 97

LLC BEGINNERS GUIDE

The Most Complete Easy-to-Follow Guide on How to Form, Manage and Maintain Your Limited Liability Company

Steven Carlson

We invite you to scan this **QR code** using the camera of your phone to access your bonus content:

SCAN THE QR CODE BELOW

INTRODUCTION

Firstly, I must congratulate you on having made a wise decision, in terms of reading this book, as opposed to diving straight into registering a Limited Liability Company (LLC), without adequate knowledge and information.

The trial-and-error method is not one that is well suited to this subject.

Many people have fantastic business acumen, but when it comes to administration, and perhaps even understanding the best way to structure an entity, for optimum profitability, and legal protection, they may lack the necessary skills.

The aim of this book is to give you a complete picture of Limited Liability Companies, so you can arm yourself with the required knowledge, to progress as effectively as possible in the business world.

I will begin with a detailed explanation of LLC's and make an initial assessment as to their suitability. Then I will move to the steps needed, to create your first LLC, in addition to the possible disadvantages.

Please remember that this book is not intend to convince you to operate your business as an LLC, and some readers may realize that an LLC is not the way to go. To that end, the contents are completely objective, and will leave you in an educated position, so as to make a decision about the best path for you.

I will look at single and multiple member LLC's and discuss the benefits of each. In simple terms, a single member LLC is less complicated, and gives you complete control. A multiple member LLC comes with more steps, more paperwork, and more requirements, in addition to the possibility of member disagreement.

A decision you will have to make is whether you want to member manage your LLC or appoint a manager. Factors such as cost and time must also be considered, and I will address those, as well as other influencing factors.

Interestingly, you can register an LLC in a state in which you do not live. That is called a foreign LLC, as opposed to a domestic LLC, which is based in your home state. I will explain further and look at what you should consider when making this decision.

There is a section on business licenses, and how they impact on your LLC, especially if you are a qualified professional, such as a lawyer or an accountant.

I will then go on to deal with series LLCs, where individuals and other LLCs can be members. These are generally used for multiple opportunity businesses, and I will unpack what that means.

Naming your entity is important, and I take time to explore the options, including DBA's, or 'Doing Business As' registration, which is often used for member anonymity, and legal protection.

You may want to convert your current business into an LLC, or vice versa, for a variety of reasons, so I will explore those, in detail.

I will take you through mistakes that can be avoided when converting your business, or forming your LLC, such as registering the wrong entity, failing to comply with regulations, and poor record keeping.

Accounting practices differ across the realm of entities, and at the end of the day, we all want to operate the most tax effective business vehicle. These topics are vitally important, and by reading this book you will learn more about structuring your finances in such a way as to minimize your dealings with the IRS, or other tax authorities.

If you are on top of your taxes, you can request that the IRS tax you as an S-corp, or C-corp, and I will explain the difference between those types of entities. Estimated tax, filed quarterly, is a very specific process, and can differ largely, especially in situations where your LLC is taxed, and so are you/other members, in your personal capacity.

It is important to define roles in your business, convene shareholders meetings, and, depending on circumstances, come up with resolutions and make decisions in annual shareholders meetings.

You need to know the tax benefits associated with deductible social security and tax deductible medicare expenses. This may be overlooked, but certainly shouldn't be, if you are wanting to optimize your tax effectiveness.

Also bear in mind that no business entity is endless, and it is a good idea to look at a sole proprietorship, company, trading structure, and the like, from a legal protection point of view.

Dissolving an LLC, for example, can be used as a business tactic, and in some instances, you can put together a six-month plan, in a hypothetical or actual sense, with the end goal of either diversifying, or downsizing. I mean as a business, not an LLC, because once dissolved the LLC no longer exists, but you can carry on your business in other ways.

It may sound a bit strange, but I have always looked at business entities as if they are people. You may have heard of natural persons, and juristic persons, and one of the objectives of LLC's is to, as the name suggests, limit your liability as a natural person, and maximize your LLC's liability as a juristic person.

I will also look at corporations, which certainly differ from LLC's, in subtle ways, but also vastly, in that the rules are stricter. You could also say that there are more rules, as each corporation has to have a board of directors that make decisions, shareholding is percentage based, and financial management is more intricate than LLC's.

Sounds confusing, but don't worry, it will become clear as you progress through this book. Just have patience, and an eager mind.

Personally, I have acted as a joint member in a not-for-profit company, and a sole member in a private industrial sector company, as well as a director and part shareholder of a parent business, registered as a corporation in the legal field.

I have made mistakes in business and learnt from them to the point where I consider myself very well-versed in the optimum use of LLC's. I am confident that, as you progress through this book, you will gain the required knowledge to be the best you can be in business.

Before I get into the nitty gritty, I would like to offer a piece of advice, which would be to take notes and make summaries as you progress through the book. When you get to the end, you can go through what you have noted and consult the particular section again for clarity and greater understanding.

Don't feel overwhelmed if you have no knowledge at all on the subject. You will learn, so proceed with an eager mind, and I will help you to be the best you can be in terms of business structure.

CHAPTER ONE

LLC'S EXPLAINED

What Exactly are LLC's and How do They Work?

Let's look at the first "L," limited, then the second L liability, by way of an example.

If you have a small car accident, a fender bender let's say, and you are at fault, then you are liable for the damage to the other driver's car. If you are insured, you are still liable, but that liability is limited. Your insurance company will pay for the damage; however, you will need to cover the collateral, also referred to as "the excess." That collateral (excess) will most likely be less than the cost to repair the other driver's vehicle, but, if you are not insured at all, you are liable for the entire repair bill.

This is just an example to illustrate the terms, "limited," and "liability," so it has nothing to do with companies, but it creates an understanding of the concept.

Ask yourself a simple question, "Do I want to be less liable, or more liable?" I am sure you will choose the former, so let's apply the concepts specifically to companies. Consider the fact that there are many people out there, who will register an LLC, but tacitly waive the personal legal protection by signing personal surety. Never do that—I will come back to this topic.

The term LLC refers specifically to companies in the U.S., so if you are in other parts of the world, the terms may be, "Proprietary Limited," or "Limited Liability Partnerships," but the structures are very similar.

Major corporations are like LLCs on steroids, and offer the same protection; however, they are intrinsically complicated, and the domain of the, "Good 'Ol Boys."

I suppose you could say that LLCs are a lay person type of entity, to be broadly colloquial.

As I said earlier, an LLC can be seen as a person, and it is very possible that an LLC can be in serious debt, but you, as a separate person but also as a member of the LLC, are not liable for one cent of the company debt. There are some exceptions, but I'll get to those in good time.

To break it down in a practical sense, let's say that a businessman by the name of Jim White, is the sole member of an LLC called JW Trading. The LLC has been in existence for 10 years, and Jim has made a comfortable living from the company. He has managed to pay off his mortgage and buy himself several vintage cars. He basically has no debt in his personal capacity.

JW Trading loses a major contract, and quickly gets into significant debt, but Jim was smart enough to make sure that JW Trading never acquired any assets whatsoever. This means that creditors can sue the pants off JW Trading, and get legal judgments against the company, but cannot repossess the company's assets because there aren't any.

Jim's liability is 100% limited, so his house and cars are safe, in addition to any other assets in his personal name. I am often asked if a wife or husband of the LLC member can be personally liable. The answer is obvious because that person has no involvement, so liability is not even up for discussion.

Back to Jim, the only issue he may face is that he no longer has an income; however, he could start another business, or sell some of his cars, to maintain a good lifestyle.

This might sound a bit unfair but remember that the legislation intends to provide personal protection, and Jim has operated within the law, so he has not done anything to compromise his morals. All he has done is operated in a smart manner, by using the benefits of an LLC.

Fundamentally, LLC's, by their very nature, offer asset protection, and in the above hypothetical case, Jim has protected his personal assets. If you want to be exact in a simple sense, you could refer to an LLC, as a "personal asset protector."

Pro's and Con's of Starting an LLC, in General

Most of us make pro and con lists, and if we don't, then we should. It is a very simple, yet effective way to assist in decision making. This is even more applicable when starting a business, and trying to work out what structure will operate most effectively, in your specific situation

Arguably the biggest pro is taxation, which differs slightly depending on the number of members of the LLC. A single member LLC, such as JW Trading, is taxed as a sole proprietorship, whereas a multiple member LLC is taxed as a partnership. These terms are basically semantics, and in very simple terms, whether there is one member, or seven members, each member is taxed in their personal capacity, but only on profits.

Consider this, general employees will often receive medical care benefits that are covered by the companies that they work for, and exactly the same applies to members of LLC's. So, the company pays, thus, personal profit is reduced and so is tax liability.

Another pro is that there are less rules, so to speak. Decision making processes are widely discretionary and members can essentially do what they like, in terms of company management and possibilities.

There are no shareholder resolutions, or meeting attendance quotas, or the need to get a whole bunch of signatures before doing anything. The private sector bureaucracy is eliminated, and nobody enjoys bureaucracy; except the damn bureaucrats, who do their best to do as little as possible, at the slowest pace possible.

Also, LLC as a suffix to your company's name, adds credibility. JW Trading, LLC sounds more professional and official than just JW Trading. I would compare it to registering your own domain, as opposed to having a Yahoo.com email address. A small pro, but a pro nonetheless.

There is also some wiggle room in terms of profit sharing, and whilst share certificates are often drafted in LLC's, they are not a requirement, so profit share agreements in multiple member LLC's can differ from month to month. It can be said to follow the old KISS analogy, Keep It Simple Stupid.

You may have started to wonder when the cons were coming…Well here they are. Cost is a potential con, and certainly depends on which state your LLC is registered in. As you can imagine, in California, the registration fees are outrageous, and on top of those, the annual renewal fees are just as bad. But taxation is also very stringent and limiting; your taxes will be high. This con is semi-mitigated, and profit declaration through large company expenditure is the silver lining.

I suppose you could say that such cons are more prevalent in some states than others, and the same applies to resignation of old members, and appointment of new members. In Michigan for instance, if a member resigns, the company has to be dissolved and re-formed, which is both ridiculous and impractical, but not the end of the world.

At this stage, and I assure you that I am maintaining objectivity, there are more pros. As a disclaimer though, your location does have a significant impact.

Advantages and Disadvantages of Single and Multiple Member LLC's

I don't need to expand much on the single/multiple terms, so it will suffice to say that some LLCs have a single member, and others have multiple members, to state the obvious. Let's look at the ramifications of both, focusing on advantages vs disadvantages.

The primary advantage, whether a single or multiple LLC is control. As a single member, you have complete control, as it is you, you, and you; that goes without saying. In a multi member LLC, control doesn't have to be guided by investment, number of votes, or by any form of hierarchical system of management. Remuneration and profit share are not subject to the stringent regulations applied to corporations.

Again, tax processes are quite simple, and every member is seen by the tax man as self-employed. Thus, the entity does not turn in corporate tax assessments, rather, the members do their own individual returns.

Personally, I feel more in control, being seen as self-employed by the state, but this can be a double-edged corporate sword when it comes to single or multiple members.

Single member means complete control and decision making. Multi-member could lead to disagreements, in terms of what to declare, or how expenses are run through the LLC. So that can be a disadvantage, but then again, as a member, you are not forced to disclose how you structure your returns.

Also bear in mind that in any business relationship, there will be all sorts of disagreements, not related to tax, so the disadvantages can be quite broad.

I have been in management positions in the past, but I found that my non-confrontational personality made it difficult to be assertive enough. So, I'd rather be a single member LLC, to maintain autonomy.

What I am trying to say is that actual business acumen isn't always the factor that these decisions turn on, and everybody always says not to make business decisions based on emotion. I agree and I don't, but you need to analyze your personality. You may favor paying more taxes and having autonomy than paying less taxes but risking professional differences, leading to toxic business relationships.

A slightly different advantage is that non-citizens can form LLC's, which is certainly not the case all over the world. Although I would argue that this is a good thing, the 'out of the box' issue could be xenophobia, but that isn't related to limiting one's liability, and I don't want to get into pseudo-politics.

The biggest disadvantage is issuing stocks to outside investors, which is prohibited by law in LLCs, and that would be a 'do not pass go' scenario.

One of my former companies, was a commodity trading LLC, that owned nothing, not even a mobile phone, and that was from a solely personal asset protection point of view. It worked well, because I was your antithetical middleman. I bought salt and rice from suppliers and delivered them to customers on flat-bed vehicles without even seeing a truck or the product.

As Bob Dylan said, in his 1978 single, 'Like a Rolling Stone,' "When you ain't got nothing, you got nothing to lose." To me, protecting myself, in my personal capacity, is the most important thing, generally, and in business. Thus, I see it as a very advantageous convention of an LLC. However, I have met people that thrive on risk, and can become addicted to the thrill of risk-taking. I kind of understand that, but I'd rather go skydiving than put my personal financial comfort on the line.

Should You Form an LLC?

It's too early to say. I encourage you to read on, but you should have a rudimentary understanding of LLCs at this juncture; however, I do implore you to get as much information as you can before deciding.

It can be compared to rushing into a romantic relationship. Early on you think that you have met your person, but as time goes by, you realize that you have made a big mistake and that the two of you are incapable of functioning as a happy couple. When you look back, you come to terms with the fact that you should have taken things slowly in the beginning. You regret that you jumped straight in before finding out whether the person's traits, habits, and disposition were compatible with you as an individual.

So, get the info, assess the viability, and make your business decision based on as much knowledge as you can gain. Read other books and articles or find YouTube videos that can help you and dispel some fears that you may have.

Don't be too hard on yourself or put excess amounts of pressure on your decisions, just avoid rushing.

Chapter Summary

Limit personal liability, or LLC's, means that a member or members' personal assets and investments are not the property of your company.

This scenario reflects the intent of the legislation, and as we have seen, legal protection is vital in any sense, but specifically when it comes to separating your LLC from yourself (or other members).

Taxation can be managed in a simple way, members are treated like self-employed individuals, and deal with the IRS as such.

To stick my neck out there, single member LLCs are not that different from multiple member LLCs, but there is the risk of disagreements.

Unlike corporations, investment, dividends, and general operation of the LLC is simpler and not subject to the strict corporate bureaucracy and regulations.

Lastly, 'knowledge' yourself up instead of making a snap decision, or an ill-informed one. Decisions about your financial future are not flippant, so, take your time and keep it as simple as possible!

CHAPTER TWO

IS IT RIGHT FOR YOUR BUSINESS?

T he only way of finding out if an LLC is your best business vehicle is to look at other types of entities in a similar way to Chapter One—compare the intricacies of different structures, tax, functionality, and personal protection, to make an informed decision.

Don't lose sight of the fact that within the realm of LLC's, there are what I would loosely term, 'sub-categories' that do differ, but for now, it is time for corporation information.

Corporations Explored

Most people have heard of John Rockefeller, the Oil magnate, and to a lesser extent, Andrew Carnegie, one of the pioneers of the industrial development of steel manufacture. These two men were important influencers on major corporation operation and the development thereof.

As an interesting fact, corporations in the U.S. became a 'thing' in the 1790's, but the Boston Manufacturing Company became the first corporation with large reach and influence when it was formed in 1813. So, corporations have been around for over 200 years, and are over 150 years older than LLC's... but older doesn't mean better.

I remain objective, so it is time to unpack the ins and outs of corporations by addressing the three main points relating to formation, operation, and individual life span.

The Structure of Corporations

When I say structure, I am using quite a broad-brush stroke that encompasses actual legal structure, but also structure in a practical and operational sense.

First off, corporations have shareholders, as opposed to members, like LLC's. The shareholders are the owners of a corporation, and ownership is determined by the number of shares held. For example, if a corporation has 100 shares, and you own 30 shares, your percentage shareholding is 30%. If you own 50 shares, your percentage shareholding is 50%, and so on.

I talked about my trading business a bit earlier and stated that it was an LLC that had no outside investors. It is not impossible to find outside investors, but it does come with its own set of risks in LLC scenarios.

Corporations are financial entities that attract outside investors. One of the reasons being that shareholding allocation, record and transfer follow a standard set of rules, which create eternal life for any corporation.

Remember that LLC's can cease to exist as I explored in Chapter One, and depending on your business goals, may lead you to favor a corporation over an LLC, or vice versa.

Requirements in the day-to-day running of corporations follow stringent rules, and it can feel like there are a lot of processes that can delay decision making, but if everyone pulls together and effectively follows the rules, then the processes can operate hastily. This is somewhat rare though.

Every important decision must be overseen by the board of directors, which is a compulsory tenet of a corporation. This type of oversight is a good thing when it comes to a thorough assessment of what is best for the corporation. The bad part is that it is often difficult to get all the directors into one room to have these types of discussions, hence the delays as mentioned above.

Annual financials must, by law, be drawn up and presented. This can be complicated and the bigger the corporation, the bigger the complication, which most often means outside auditors, who don't come cheap. If you are like me, and prefer feeling that you have complete control, a corporation probably will not work for you.

Taxation, when it comes to corporations, is more complicated and cynics refer to 'double taxation,' meaning that the corporation is taxed on profits, and shareholders are taxed on dividends.

To some, it makes sense, to others, it is just the IRS taking the mickey. I will explore this factor in detail in Chapter Eight, but I think it is safe to say that NOBODY wants to get the runaround by the IRS.

I must again remind you of my objectivity, but for arguments sake, let's say you are favoring LLCs at this point—then you need to gain some knowledge. Here we go!

Different Types of LLC's

Now that you have an understanding of corporations and how they differ from LLC's, let's change focus to the differences between different LLC's.

Certain types of LLC's do overlap, but still maintain legal separation between member and company. Hence the taxation as an individual.

You already know what single member and multiple member LLCs are and how they operate, broadly speaking, so on we go to the other types. Before I get there, I must mention that not all states recognize every type of LLC, but you can register most types of LLCs in most states.

Member-Managed LLC

I'm not a fan of the term 'one-man-band,' but it is appropriate in this case. If your business is small, you probably want to manage and run it on your own. In any case, if you are just getting your business going, you don't want to be wasting part of your initial start-up and running costs.

You will wear many hats—coffee maker, accountant, repair person, sales expert, and many more. The moral is, just do it... yourself. Be cautious though, don't keep banging your head against the wall, trying to do things out of your scope.

Also consider that if your LLC becomes highly successful very quickly, you probably won't be able to do everything yourself; in which case, help is available, it is just about finding the right person for the job.

Manager-Managed LLC

Let's take the example of a food outlet or restaurant. You absolutely have to have staff, and I haven't come across too many restaurants that are owner-member managed, although there are some around. I guess your smaller, boutique type restaurants, or outlets that only serve breakfast and lunch, can be owner managed.

If your restaurant is open from 8 a.m. to 10 p.m. though, and you member-manage, soon you will become exhausted, but if you appoint a competent manager, you can focus on the areas of the business that require your attention as a single member.

A quick tip, when you hire a manager, or any staff member for that matter, you need to be thorough, from paying attention to the resume to contacting previous employers, to discuss the potential employee's references. The interview is also important, and that human connection is too. If you are uncomfortable in any way with a potential manager, then carry on looking.

Domestic LLC

This refers to an LLC in a particular state, and you could say that the LLC 'lives' in XYZ-state. So, XYZ-state is then said to be the 'domicile' or residence, being the legal terms for your LLC's home, so to speak.

Just a quick reminder that an LLC is a person, i.e., a juristic one, and its members are natural persons. These are not steadfast terms, but you get what I mean.

Foreign LLC

Not all LLCs operate in one state only, and may have offices or factories in various states, alternatively they may just generate income from deals concluded in other states. This is an example of an overlap because this type of LLC is registered as domestic in one state and foreign in the others, in which it conducts business.

Professional Limited Liability Company

If you are a professional license holder, such as a doctor or an accountant, you are pretty much restricted to this type of LLC, whether it is single or multiple members—so another small overlap.

You may elect to be regarded as an S Corporation for tax effective purposes to minimize self-employment tax burdens. I will delve into taxation in more depth later in this book; it is important!

Series LLC's

I would say that this is my least favorite type of LLC, and there are a good few states that agree with me. My thinking is that if you want to make your entity an LLC, for simplicity, then Series won't work for you.

You have an umbrella LLC, with other LLC's below it, operating completely separately, in terms of rights, obligations, debts, and taxation. I guess I am being a little subjective here, but again, the choice is yours, I am just giving opinions and information.

Stay tuned for more.

What to Consider When Choosing a Type of LLC

A lot of successful businesspeople will tell you that they went by their gut, or that they followed a hunch, in making a vital decision. That is all good and well, but I would apply these 'sixth sense type' emotions to a deal, or an idea to find a new niche. Choosing the right way to do those things, in terms of your entity type, should be a more measured consideration.

There are a fair number of factors that can guide your decision to choose the LLC that works best for you.

Number of Members

I don't want to repeat myself too much, but I do need to in order to ensure that you are reminded of all elements. This is very important.

Single LLC members enjoy legal protection in their personal capacities and are taxed as an individual… so are multiple members though, thus the choice here would be directed towards your venture, in a personal sense.

Whether there is one member or a gazillion, each member is taxed as an individual.

Everyday Functions of Members

The choice here is member-management or manager-management and would depend on your availability and start-up capital. Maybe you have investment properties and draw a significant income there from, so you can invest a large sum in a new LLC and can afford a manager from day one. On the other hand, if you have limited funds and have to save every which way you can, then your natural choice would be member-management.

Sometimes the choice isn't easy, and you may have to relinquish a bit of immediate control for the financial growth of your LLC. There are of course systems that you can put in place to monitor a manager's performance, which is important in any employer/employee scenario.

Should you Register Your LLC as Domestic or Foreign?

If you intend on creating a multi-state LLC then foreign is your option, but don't forget that it will be domestic to the initial state. This factor depends entirely on the type of business: If you open a restaurant in one state, and have no interest in creating a chain, or even opening independent restaurants in other states, then a domestic LLC is perfect for you. If your goal is to have restaurants in multiple states, then a foreign LLC is more suited to you.

Are the Members Licensed Professionals?

There are many careers that require a professional license, and you will, of course, know that you have that license, depending on your field of expertise. So, this is quite a simple one when it comes to choosing the best LLC, which in this scenario would be a Professional Limited Liability Company.

With professional licenses comes the risk of being sued for malpractice, but if there are multiple members in these types of LLCs, only the member being sued for malpractice can attract liability. To put it more simply, if you require a professional license you have to form a PLLC (if you want to steer away from a corporation, which is probably your best bet as a professional).

Take note that if you have changed vocations, and even though you have a professional license, you are no longer operating in that field, then you are unable to form an PLLC. For example, a former doctor starts a furniture manufacturing business. No license is required, so a PLCC no longer applies. Basically, that option is no longer there, and perhaps makes the decision an easier one.

Is the Point of the LLC to Create Multiple Opportunities?

This choice can be made using two examples that are suited to series LLCs, and you could even treat the term 'series' as one that also means multiple… sort of.

Multiple Restaurants

To put it very simply, let's say someone chokes on a bone in one of your restaurants, your other two restaurants cannot be held liable. It might sound obvious, and no offense to the legislators, but the law really has left the door open wide for ridiculous suits.

Rental Properties

You own three apartment complex properties. If there is an air conditioner in one of the units, and it falls on your tenant and they get injured, your other two properties attract zero liability. Again, sounds obvious, but the things people litigate over leaves one aghast from time to time.

Chapter Summary

Corporations differ from LLCs in that they have a stricter framework and set of rules.

LLC's have members, whereas corporations have shareholders who are seen as the owners of whatever corporation it may be. That percentage ownership is dependent on how many shares each owner holds (50% share = 50% ownership).

Corporations have directors, and decision making is subject to board of director meetings. This extra oversight does make sense because most often corporations are largely funded by investors, who entrust the board to make the correct decisions.

On the accounting side, annual financials have to be produced, which can be complicated and require outside, independent auditors.

In terms of LLC's specifically, your circumstances will dictate whether you will be a single member or a multi member. If you have restricted capital and choose to be a single member, your LLC will be member managed. The same applies to multiple members, and an option if you are flexible in terms of capital, you may want to appoint a manager.

If you want to operate in one state, then you will favor a domestic LLC, and if your business is run in multiple states, you will use a foreign LLC.

Professionally licensed individuals are inevitably going to set up Professional Limited Liability Companies.

Series LLCs are suited to multiple opportunity businesses, and the examples I gave were real estate and restaurant ownership, where each entity making up the multiple opportunity LLC is exempt from legal responsibility attached to the other entities.

So, there are the choices, but before we press on, if you have the feeling that you have been bombarded with too much information, I recommend flicking through this chapter and Chapter One again to make notes and consolidate your understanding.

CHAPTER THREE

STARTING AN LLC

I am not one for administration or for reading instructions properly. You can imagine how I approach putting together an Ikea table.

These traits are not good when it comes to starting a business entity, so my recommendation is to take the required steps slowly, and don't start thinking that you know what to do before you know how to do it. It's kind of like saying, "Make sure that you read the instructions."

The Seven Steps

Step One: Choosing a Name

This is important for many reasons, and the first obvious one is that you need to have the kind of name that will get your business noticed.

From a purely personal perspective, I would avoid names like, "Gloves 4 U," or "Guitars 'R Us." They sound cheesy and are definitely overused; but in their defense, you know what you are going to get.

There are lots of considerations, and I would urge you to write down and ponder over some options before you check if there are existing LLC's with the name that you are set on.

Avoid anything controversial and don't use profanity in the title. Don't have any sexual, political, or religious connotations to your name. I once saw a company called, "Trust in God Trucking," and I will admit that it does have a ring to it, but you may chase away people with different beliefs.

You don't want a name that is difficult to pronounce, as you don't want potential customers saying, "Pardon? Could you please say that again?"

Get onto google and look at businesses similar to yours, see what kind of names they use, and get a guideline.

Shortly after I left college, I very stupidly started an LLC called BC Souring and Distribution. The name does not tell you what the business does, and it's awkward to say. However, in certain circumstances, you may want this to be the situation. I could have decided to go into industry, and call my LLC, BG Precision Window Glazing; easy to say, easy to remember, no doubt about what service the company provides.

There can also be personal influences involved. For instance, there is a company called "Bud's Biscuits" in an industrial area close to where I live. The owner's first family dog was named "Bud" and fits the title well.

I have not yet mentioned registering a 'Doing Business As,' called a DBA for short, so let's get to it.

Whether you have a single member LLC, or are a member of a multiple member LLC, you may want to avoid using your name or the names of your fellow members as part of your business name.

As an aside, but also as an explanation, in certain countries you can buy shelf companies, and form a 'trading as' entity. So, the name of the shelf company may be, "A and S Services" for instance, but you are a plumbing business, so you could call the business, "Mark Wright Tip Top Plumbing." The full name will be, "A and S Services, trading as, Mark Wright Tip Top Plumbing," but you are only required to use "Mark Wright Tip Top Plumbing" on your signage, company docs, business cards, etc.

People actually make money out of registering companies with common names that businesses may require. The company doesn't actually trade, but if you want to use that specific name, you can buy the shelf company—but you are essentially buying the name.

You can look at the DBA registration as an opposite of the Mark Wright scenario. You want to maintain anonymity as far as possible, whereas Mark wants his name out there in the public. When registering a DBA, you can quite literally make up any name, as long as it is not yet taken, which is a good idea, especially if your industry niche is extremely specific and there is significant risk involved.

What I am getting at is that by registering a DBA, you do not have to use your name or the names of your fellow members on signage, letterheads, and the like. You could go with, "Onboard Enterprizes," or "PG Management," or whatever else suits your fancy.

Step Two: Appointing a Registered Agent

A registered agent is the person who receives legal and/or financial documents and notices on behalf of the LLC and passes such onto the person or people in charge.

You can appoint yourself, another member of the LLC, an employee, or your auditors if the appointee is available during business hours in the state where your LLC is registered.

A company, such as a law firm or accounting firm, can be registered as an agent, which is only necessary if your LLC expands quickly.

The appointment of a company requires an annual fee, different in every state, but not more than a couple hundred dollars annually.

Step Three: Obtaining the Articles of Organization Form

These forms are referred to by different names in different states, so don't be afraid to call the form the wrong thing. That is a very small issue. You can find the form on your state authorities' website and download it for completion, before returning it by way of upload, email, or hand delivery.

Step Four: Preparing the Articles of Association Form

The information required is your name if you are a single member, otherwise all the names of members in a multi-member LLC, their places of residence, and the principal business address.

You will also need to complete a section detailing the purpose of the business, how it will be managed, and the intended duration of operation.

Lastly, the registered agent's details are required, from which point you can submit the form to your state authority.

In certain states you need to publish a notice stating that you will be registering an LLC. This must obviously be done prior to completing the articles of organization form.

Step Five: Filing the Articles of Association Form

When you file the form, no matter the method, you will be required to pay a filing fee; the amount of which is state dependent.

You will then be issued with a registration certificate, which is the documents that banks will need you to produce, so that the LLC can open a business bank account.

When obtaining a tax number, the registered certificate is needed, so make a few copies, have them certified, and keep them in a safe place.

Future customers or suppliers may request to see the certificate before entering into credit agreements, so don't think that you will never need it after registration of your LLC.

Step Six: The Operating Agreement

This agreement should be very specific, even more so if you are creating a multiple member LLC. Think of it like the rules to a game or sport, you must follow them. They are not compulsory in every state, but I would advise any LLC to create one anyway.

Look at it like a business plan that you would present, so include specifics as to operational management, capital investment, and profit share. Also use the agreement to define roles and procedures for effective day-to-day running.

Even if it is a single member LLC, you have to have a plan, or at the very least, a framework around which your plan is built. An accountant or an attorney could assist you in drawing up the agreement, but there are a plethora of templates that you can find on the internet, if you would like to do it yourself.

Step Seven: Keep Your LLC Alive

Take note of the requirements in your state, some LLCs have to pay renewal fees every year, others pay bi-annually. Some states require reports, others don't.

If changes are made to your LLC, you need to inform the state authority. It would be a disaster if you lost a big supply contract, for instance, because you forgot to tick a small box.

Treat your business like a person, and do the things needed to keep that person happy, healthy, and functional.

Before I turn to business-friendly states that you should consider when registering your LLC, I would like to address, and give some tips on, something that will likely prove vital in the setting up and early trading stages of your LLC... the money.

Business Credit

It is exceptionally difficult to run any business without some form of credit facility, so I would strongly recommend exploring different credit options. You can get revolving loans, periodical repayment credit, overdraft facilities, outside financiers, even interest free loans from generous family members. If you can get a good structure going, you can utilize business credit to your advantage. I'd like to put forward a scenario that is not unrealistic, but one that takes planning and negotiating.

You can't avoid your standard banking fees, and whilst they differ from institution to institution, the range is similar, but you can minimize interest by holding funds for as long as possible.

Many credit offering institutions have packages where they charge minimal interest if you pay up your accounts within 30 days of creating credit. A revolving loan is a good example. You have access to $20,000 at any time, and your interest rate is 5%, but if you top up that account/loan within 30 days, you are charged 1%.

What you want to do is have agreements with customers, to whom you have given credit, whereby they pay your account within 20 days from statement. You can then hold that money for one week to ten days and top up the loan account within the 30-day period to minimize your interest. So, you are getting interest off your customer/s money, which is held in your business account, for your week to ten days, and reducing your interest payable by servicing your revolving loan within the 1%-time frame. It is less complicated than it sounds, you just have to arrange and plan effectively. But consider that this is the optimum scenario, so don't get discouraged.

A small tip is to do some research on credit providers and not just decide on a bank before visiting several banks, or finance houses, and understand their different offerings.

Which State(s) to File Your Operating Agreement in

Interestingly, you can set up your LLC in a state that it does not operate from. Having said that, it is much more effective to register your LLC in the state in which you live.

Either way, you will have to file requisite paperwork, tax returns, and the like in your home state, so think of the practicality before you register; however, don't discount financial effectiveness when registering your LLC out of state.

Filing in Your Home State

This is based on convenience. You are more than likely familiar with the laws and regulations in your state, the different governmental branches and their location, as well as contacts that can advise and assist.

Consider the physical site of your business and where most of the trading is done. If the answer to these two considerations is the state that you live in, then practicality dictates filing in that state.

If your business operates in more than one state, it will have to be registered as a domestic LLC and a foreign LLC. These days, remote work is so common that this type of registration has become more popular. There is always the cost factor though. If you register in a foreign state, you will either have to travel there regularly in the set-up process or appoint a representative to do it for you.

Once more, it depends on your individual business circumstances.

Filing in a Foreign State

I am obviously aware that readers are likely to live all over the country, so I will look at three states in which to register an LLC, but you can investigate your home state regulations at the correct department.

The reason for looking at the following three states is due to their business friendliness, tax implications, and simplicity of structure.

Delaware

This state is very popular when registering a foreign LLC, largely because it has a reputation for being business-friendly, and that is vital if you are not going to be present.

Another reason is the Chancery Court, dedicated to business disputes only, which lends itself to streamlining matters and reaching faster resolution, than in a general court.

In addition, judges on the bench in the Chancery Court are experts in business, compared to judges in general courts, as they sit in a variety of different matters, opening themselves up to poor judgments.

Delaware does not tax out-of-state income, so if a large part of your business operations, income, and expenditure fall in a foreign state, your LLC is exempt in Delaware.

Nevada

There is no business income tax in Nevada, nor capital gains or franchise tax, which is no doubt a big advantage, especially for franchised LLC's. There is a small downside, which is the fees, and requirements for obtaining a business license and the annual filing fees. Tax vs fees is the basis for your decision.

I talked about operating agreements and how they often complicate things. In Nevada, they are not required, nor are annual meetings.

If you want to remain anonymous as far as possible, then take note of the fact that Nevada does not have an information sharing agreement with the IRS. To me, the IRS must stay out of your activities, other than actual tax related matters.

Wyoming

Wyoming is catching up to Delaware as a business-friendly state. There is no business or franchise tax, and processes are becoming more streamlined.

A convention in Wyoming when it comes to LLC's is something called lifetime proxy, which means that you, as a single member, or you and your partners, as a multiple member LLC, can appoint a representative to handle the administrative affairs.

This approach would work if you have other business operations, or if you don't have time to do justice to your participation. Total anonymity is the major benefit here, but that becomes irrelevant if you don't have a problem with, let's say, being visible.

States That are Disadvantageous to Register Your LLC

The worst of the worst is New Jersey because taxes are high, percentage wise, but also because there are virtually no tax breaks. Even setting up your LLC is expensive, so this is one to avoid.

In California, individual and corporate tax are not pocket friendly considering that the unemployment rate and general cost of living are substantially higher than in other states.

It basically comes down to cost and viability, which go hand in hand. New York for instance isn't LLC tax friendly, and the set-up costs are high.

Minnesota, Ohio, and Maryland are all high tax states when it comes to LLCs, and there are many more that are way less favorable than Delaware, Nevada, and Wyoming.

You will need to do some research on this one. The different regulatory bodies in each state are obliged to provide you with cost and tax information, so that may be a good start.

Do I Need a Lawyer to Register my LLC?

It is not a legal requirement that a lawyer attend to the registration, but it is not a bad option if you can find a lawyer with the right expertise.

My advice would be to avoid this route, as lawyers have been known to charge as much as $5,000 for this service, which to me is absolutely ridiculous! I am not saying that every lawyer charges that much, but I would not pay such outrageous fees for something I can do myself.

This book is designed to help you understand the processes, and generally the relevant state departments are very helpful, especially if you can show that you have tried to educate yourself on LLC's.

My advice would be to book a consultation with a business lawyer, hear what that person has to say, and then make a call.

A lawyer may be needed at a later stage, if your LLC grows quickly, and there are labor or litigation issues, or anything else that you feel you don't have the expertise to handle yourself.

Short answer don't hire a lawyer unless you have to.

Chapter Summary

Once you decide on a name, you need to make a call as to whether you want to appoint an agent, but for these purposes let's say that you are setting up the LLC on your own.

Get the requisite forms from the specific state authority, fill in all details. Look at it like a business plan. When you are done, make several copies, then file the forms.

The extra copies will come in handy when you need to open a bank account, deal with tax or franchise agreements, amongst others.

It is advisable to draft an operating agreement, detailing the functional running of your LLC. Make sure you are aware of any annual submission requirements and fulfill them when the time comes.

Look at the benefits of registering your LLC in a foreign state, be they simplicity, tax efficacy, or anonymity. Do some investigating into states other than the three in this chapter, to help make your mind up.

Finally, avoid lawyers or other representatives; this book should arm you with the knowledge to proceed on your own. When I say avoid, I don't mean when you really need assistance, but avoid as much as possible if you are confident in your own abilities.

CHAPTER FOUR

COMMON PITFALLS WHEN STARTING AN LLC

I t is vital to know and identify the good and the bad in order to follow the good and avoid the bad. Don't get too discouraged, these pitfalls, as the title suggests, happen often. So all you need to do is understand what they are and steer away from them.

Keep in mind that the sailing won't always be smooth, things will go wrong, that's just life, but if you can prepare for them, then you are on the right track.

I will go into S-Corps in this chapter, which are not actually LLCs, but for good reason. I will also delve deeper into taxation and thresholds.

Six Very Common Pitfalls

Choosing the Wrong Entity

Single member LLCs provide an easy set up. There aren't piles of paperwork, taxation is simple, and your personal liability is completely protected.

Tax wise, you will need to file quarterly returns, but are taxed as an individual on profits. You do have the option of requesting the IRS to tax you as an S-Corp, but why would you do that? To save tax, of course!

If your LLC makes an annual profit of $80,000 USD or more, the taxation as an S-Corp makes sense. You will have to adhere to stricter rules and regulations, such as paying yourself a salary, so you can structure your LLC in the most tax effective manner.

If your LLC is turning an annual profit of $20,000 USD, it would be a very bad decision to ask the IRS to tax you as an S-Corp, because you will end up paying more tax than if you were taxed as an individual.

This is something that you may want to take some additional financial advice on before committing.

Choosing the Wrong State in Which to Register

I referred to Delaware, Nevada, and Wyoming as business-friendly states for several reasons, but largely legal and taxation based. Now, for single member LLCs, or even multiple member LLC's, incorporating a small business may not be worth the trouble.

The inconvenience may not be worth the tax savings and remember that you have to have a representative in the foreign state. That representative's fees may negate the benefits, so a large LLC is more likely to explore multi-state registration.

Again, I say this: keep it simple as far as reasonably possible.

Becoming Non-Compliant

Overlooking something, or neglecting to follow proper practices, even if it is something really small, can cast your LLC into non-compliance, which is not good for your reputation or your LLC's pocket.

Compliance differs from state to state, but the four fundamentals are as follows:

1. Use your business name in all documents, with LLC as the suffix in every case. It adds professionalism and credibility.
2. Know what the annual reporting rules are and submit reports in line therewith.
3. If there are any changes to your LLC, such as appointing additional members, you must submit the necessary amendment forms, most often referred to as articles of amendment.
4. DO NOT mix up business funds and personal funds, you may unintentionally open yourself up to IRS scrutiny.

It is also advisable to plan for future uncertain events, such as the passing of a member in a multiple LLC or sale of the business. A simple agreement recording these types of things is strongly recommended.

Forming an LLC Without the Requisite Licenses

There isn't too much to be said about this one. You should know what business license you require, say a real estate license or license to operate, as a financial planner. Get your ducks in a row on this one, you wouldn't want your business to crumble for such a small lack of compliance.

If you are going into a new line of business, let's say construction, there will be a lot of compliance requirements, and whilst you may not require licenses specifically, you will definitely need to follow safety procedures and have compliance certificates awarded.

Do a bit of homework into what your business requires in this regard, and make sure that you do things correctly.

Not Getting the Correct Legal Assistance

As I have said before, using a lawyer to set up your LLC is not necessary, but if you feel more comfortable appointing a lawyer, then go for it. You are more likely to really need legal assistance after setting up your LLC, depending on the complexities of your business. If you want to request that the IRS tax your LLC as an S-Corp, then a lawyer is recommended.

Peace of mind is so important, in business as in life, and if hiring a lawyer to sort out multiple state registration, tax compliance, and all the paperwork in between, will give you peace of mind, then you have your answer right there.

Using Incorrect Documentation

The internet is a gift and a curse because there are unquantified amounts of standard form documents that you can download. The problem is that you need to get your hands on the correct template or set of forms that you require in a specific situation.

This is quite easy to get around, and more often than not, you can get what you require from the state department's website or physically from the department.

If your LLC expands, then you may require different licenses, labor compliance certificates, or safety standard documents. Make sure you do your homework and never presume that you have downloaded the correct form(s). Rather, do your checks and get that peace of mind; alternatively, get some assistance.

Mistakes to Avoid When Running an LLC

If you are a first-time business owner, you must be aware of things that you perhaps would not otherwise have thought of as an employee. Getting your LLC into debt is a massive mistake made all the time. Take as little money as you can out of your LLC, even if your business gets off to a very lucrative start. The idea is to build up a fund that you can draw from in the hard times, the best example of which is Covid-19. Nobody could have foreseen the pandemic, but it happened.

This doesn't mean that you can't have accounts with your customers, suppliers, and service providers as long as you ensure that your cash flow is sufficient. Do background checks into every person or business that you have dealings with during your set-up phase, and make this a habit from day one. When you do business with a new company or individual in the future, that habit should be ingrained in you.

Don't spend company money unnecessarily. If you have an office, you don't need top of the range furniture if your LLC is just starting up. Make sure that your bookkeeping is on point, and that you have oversight of the business operations, day to day. Avoid saying, "I'll just take it out of petty cash." There have to be systems in place, and even if you are a single member LLC, you have to follow the rules that you set for yourself.

Let's look a little closer at four specific potential mistakes.

Not Having a Deadlock Provision in the Operating Agreement

The legal term for a deadlock provision is an 'Impasse Resolution,' and it addresses, well, a deadlock, when making decisions in multiple member LLC's. Don't worry about the legal name, I will use 'deadlock provision.'

For instance, if a four member LLC requires outside finance, and there are two different financial institutions that could grant credit, the four members will vote. If the votes are deadlocked at 2/2, then there has to be a way of finalizing the decision, and the operating agreement will be called upon in such circumstances.

As an example, using the above scenario, the deadlock clause may allow member two to make a final decision, based on the fact that member two has the best knowledge and understanding as to how financiers operate. It makes sense to allow the most informed member to hold the swing vote.

This applies to any decision whatsoever, and if there is no provision in the agreement, the decision-making process could get ugly and complicated.

The Operating Agreement is Outdated

Laws do change from time to time and may require your LLC to amend its operating agreement. It doesn't mean that your business plan has to be changed, just added to, and may even be subtracted from.

If you are not up to speed with the legal requirements in your state, or in foreign states for that matter, and another company litigates against you for non-compliance, if picked up by the other companies, lawyers may put your LLC in a position of disadvantage. Never forget though, that your personal liability is protected, so in this type of situation, things would be way worse without that protection.

Members Do Not Properly Document LLC Activity

This is very common, often because members want to attend to the running of the LLC. At the end of the day, money making work can seem more important than administration, but maintaining records could save your bacon, for these next few reasons.

Keeping Proper Records Offers Greater Legal Protection

If a lawsuit arises, the opposing attorneys will try to discredit your LLC by alleging that record keeping paperwork is not in order. The idea is to then come after your personal assets based on a technicality.

This isn't always the case, and in a situation where your LLC is bankrupt, lawyers probably won't even bother coming after you because you have the protection that is limited liability.

Drafting a Memorandum in Order to Record Percentage Shares

You would not want to think that your ownership percentage is 25%, and later discover that it has not been recorded in writing if a dispute arises with your business partners.

Even if you go into business with your best friend, you should still draw up the memorandum as people can fall out. You are protecting every member by doing the memorandum, so don't neglect to draft it.

Defining Management Roles

Again, this should be in writing, so everybody involved has clarity as to what their individual roles are, and in the case of confusion for any reason, the management role documents can be consulted.

Look at it like job descriptions and business policies, written down, filed, but hopefully not needed.

Documenting Contributions and Loans

If there comes a time to take money out of your LLC, and there is no record of what you put in, you may face a big problem. The same would apply to personal loans taken from company funds. Keep these records up to date! But as I have said, avoid touching company funds.

Just to clarify, members can borrow from the LLC against their loan accounts, which would not qualify as mixing business and personal transactions.

Transfer of Assets

If your LLC buys assets, you need to draw up and keep sale agreements so that you can account for what your LLC owns, if need be. This would apply in a bankruptcy situation, for instance, in which you would have to transfer assets to creditors, or sell them, to raise money owed.

Mixing Company Funds With Personal Funds

This is a big no no! You must never use company funds for personal expenses, or vice versa. It just muddies the waters and can lead to disputes between members. Don't do it, not even once.

Just think about the possibility of a good business relationship turning sour because of something like this, which should be easy to control. Absolute necessity may arise, but only in extreme circumstances should you go against this rule.

Note, that members loaning the entity money does not qualify as mixing personal and business funds. Members have loan accounts; this is very normal.

Chapter Summary

Record keeping and doing things by the book are the themes in this chapter, and you need to do this to cater for something that may come to light in the future where producing records will settle a dispute.

You need to choose the entity that is most effective, especially in terms of tax, so requesting that the IRIS tax you as a C-Corp isn't wise, unless your turnover is significant enough to create tax benefits.

Legal compliance is obviously vital, and for this reason you don't want to get the wrong legal advice or neglect to apply for the correct licenses.

Record everything in writing so as to avoid disputes and to cover yourself and your LLC in the case of litigation, IRS scrutiny, and day to day running policies.

It may seem a bit overwhelming, but if you break it down step by step, you will be fine.

CHAPTER FIVE

CONVERTING YOUR EXISTING BUSINESS INTO AN LLC

This may sound like something quite challenging, and it is to a certain extent, but probably not as much as you might think. Perhaps you jumped straight in and just started operating your business as yourself, otherwise referred to as a sole proprietorship, and you have come to realize that an LLC offers you more protection and tax advantages than a sole proprietorship.

Maybe your business has grown significantly, or you have been awarded a big contract, which will increase expenditure (and hopefully profits). Looking into converting that business into an LLC, and once again, limiting your personal liability, would be very viable.

There could be a situation in which converting your business to an LLC may not be viable; however, you will only know that if you explore the options and possibilities, which I will deal with in this chapter.

At this stage of the book, you should have a conceptual understanding of LLCs, so you have an advantage off the bat. Before I continue, I need to mention that conversions are not possible in all states.

What Kind of Businesses Can Be Converted Into LLC's?

The specific entities that can form a new LLC or become members of an existing LLC are sole proprietorships, corporations, and LLC groups, also called parent companies in a conversion sense.

Banks, public financiers, insurance companies, medical protection companies, and several others cannot legally form or be part of LLCs for various reasons, which I am not going to go into. For these purposes they are irrelevant.

Sole Proprietorship

This one is pretty simple, as a sole proprietor is just one person, so for all intents and purposes, a brand-new LLC is formed by following the usual processes.

Articles of organization have to be filed with the relevant state department. The processes are very similar from state to state. I would encourage you to refer to the requirements, as discussed in previous chapters, although I do explore them again in what follows.

Corporation

Articles of organization also have to be filed, but first the corporation must be dissolved. Its assets are said to collapse into the LLC, which can be looked at like a transfer or sale in loose terms. The decision to convert to an LLC is made via shareholder majority vote, which may involve long meetings and discussions.

LLC Groups

This is closer to the sole proprietorship method where existing LLC's became partners in a new LLC, or an LLC that has been newly formed. Articles of organization must be filed in accordance with state laws where the business resides. It may get slightly complicated in multiple state LLC registration, but break it down step by step, use this book, and take outside advice if needed.

Advantages and Disadvantages of Changing Your Business to an LLC

There are advantages and disadvantages to every decision, and they depend on the situation, so I will go through them to allow you to weigh up the pros and cons. Practically, pros and cons may differ from person to person, so take note of that. Just because I call it a con, it may have no effect on you or your business, which would make it 'a nothing.'

A couple of things that can slow down processes are directors' meetings and shareholders meetings, which are dispensed with, after conversion to an LLC. Resolutions are also a requirement when making and recording decisions in a corporation, and the rigidity thereof is not present in LLC's.

You will notice a difference in streamlining your business, making faster decisions, and in tax related matters. Converting into an LLC, as I have mentioned, has tax implications, so moving assets into the LLC is seen by the law as a liquidation of those assets, or a sale of those assets. Those two terms are closely related, and the example I am going to give illustrates only the transfer, it has nothing to do with corporations or LLCs.

Let's assume for these purposes that you are a natural person (individual), and you sell your assets to another natural person (individual). This may be by way of a sale agreement or liquidation proceedings, but the moral of the story is that ownership changes.

The corporation is referred to as a juristic person, as is the LLC, so person one (corp) transfers its assets to person two (LLC), by sale agreement or liquidation, just like the natural person scenario.

Just as tax implications can be an advantage, they can also be a disadvantage in certain scenarios in the asset transfer realm. If the assets are valued quite highly and a 'gain' is made on them, then corporation tax will apply, as well as shareholders tax, so the streamlining that I mentioned earlier may have to be sacrificed in order to save tax.

Tax experts can give great advice on the ramifications of conversions, and how to structure asset transfer to minimize tax. I do recommend this strongly, even if it is a bit costly. Don't be penny wise, but pound foolish.

Procedure to Convert Your Sole Proprietorship to an LLC

This can be fun in a way and exciting, perhaps a new start even! There are six easy steps that can be followed, well not easy, just less complicated.

Confirm the Name of Your Business

There may be an LLC that has the same name as your sole proprietorship, so you need to investigate that through your relevant state authority. If the name is available, great! If not, you will have to come up with a new name.

If you want to be thorough, you should get in touch with the United States Patent and Trademark Office to check that you are not infringing on a trademark. Take note of what I covered in the naming section, found in Chapter Three.

File Articles of Organization

You should remember, as discussed earlier, that this document records the business details, i.e. name, address, contact, purpose of business, member or manager managed etc. If you are using an agent, that person's details must form part of the articles of organization, but an agent is not absolutely necessary, although they can be useful.

Draft Your Operating Agreement

This is not compulsory, but highly advisable to prevent disputes in the future. The agreement is between LLC members, and the idea is for everyone to be clear on operating processes, requirements, and designated roles in the business. Having this agreement in place should make everyone comfortable, know what is expected, and able to proceed confidently.

Tax Compliance

Contact the IRS to check what you need to submit in terms of tax. In a lot of states, the submission will be exactly the same as that required from a sole proprietorship, but it must be done as an LLC. Don't worry, I address tax in more detail in future chapters.

Open a Bank Account

This needs no explanation, but I would say that you should do some investigating into which banks are more viable than others. Charges, administration fees, drawing fees, card fees, and all the other damn fees, differ from bank to bank. There are banks that have tailored accounts for businesses, depending on several factors. The cheapest isn't always the best, so do your research into the financial viability vs the quality of service.

Remember that banks are not going to open an account for an entity or person that lacks credibility, so when you are presenting your business details, you don't want to have your credibility questioned.

Have all information at your disposal, don't use a post office box address, rather have a fixed address. These days everybody uses Google to investigate, so if you have used a random domicile for your LLC, it won't look good in the eyes of the bank.

It is a good idea to set up a website, a very basic one at first, which you can direct the banker who is performing due diligence to, which is a huge step in establishing credibility.

If you can get your LLC to a point where you could do a big launch, get involved in a marketing campaign, or promote your business publicly before you open your bank account, then I am certain that your LLC will not encounter any issues.

Apply for Your Business License

Depending on your industry and state, you may require a business license, so locate the correct authority and fill out the application. If you are unsure, which would be concerning, you should contact the body which has authority of your particular profession.

Procedure to Convert Your Corporation to an LLC

At the risk of getting repetitive, each state is different, but the procedures have a lot of similarities, so here is the general approach.

Create a Conversion Plan

Prepare your conversion plan, including information on current shareholders voting, assets, and meetings of the board of directors, then submit to the correct regulatory authority.

Shareholder Approval is Required

As there may be several shareholders, approval is important and the board will very likely take a vote and produce a resolution, confirming approval (or not). Without approval there is not much that can be done, but shareholders are expected to act measuredly, and delve into all factors before putting the potential conversion to the vote.

File the Correct Documents

I have discussed this extensively, so I won't go into it again, but just remember to get your document ducks in a row, and deliver them to the relevant state authority. It will only be to your advantage.

Procedure to Use Your LLC as a Member of Another LLC

This is referred to as creating a subsidiary LLC, and the set-up process is almost identical to setting up an LLC with multiple natural persons as members. The articles of association must have all the usual details, plus the details of what we call the parent company.

The parent company becomes a member of the new LLC, which can have several parent companies and natural persons as members. Obviously, somebody has to sign on behalf of the parent company, and it is very important to put your designation below your signature. It could be "company owner," "owner/manager," "president," or "executive." The title doesn't matter, but the signature on behalf of the company is the important bit.

Once you have completed the articles of association, I would recommend finding out about what business licenses the parent company and the new LLC require, then make the necessary applications if you have not yet done so.

For your own protection, you can draw up your operating agreement which defines everyone's roles. Make sure that you cross all the 't's' and dot all the 'i's' when it comes to record keeping, tax compliance, business operations, and anything that may be of use in the future, as is the case with the other entities discussed.

You often find that this structure is used for rapidly expanding businesses, and most businesses want to expand.

Chapter Summary

Converting a business to an LLC can be done for many reasons. Before you start, check that you are able to do so in your home state or another state that you have been considering.

You may be a sole proprietor, a shareholder in a corporation, or a member of an existing LLC, and your reasons for conversion may be growth, tax breaks, or even correcting a mistake in choosing the wrong entity in the beginning, perhaps too hastily. The reasons aren't important, but the correct implementation of due process is vital.

From choosing a name, to producing articles of organization, drafting operating agreements, finding out about the role of the IRS, and business structure for optimum and effective running of your entity, nothing should be neglected.

Converting a sole proprietorship is the simplest, and although corporation conversion has more steps, such as shareholders meetings and resolutions, if you follow the steps one by one, things will go smoothly. Take into consideration liquidation and/or sale of assets, the impact on tax, and the implications thereafter, before you decide.

Making an LLC into a member of an LLC is seen as a parent company becoming part of an already existing LLC, and the same advice applies to business licenses, articles of organization, operating agreements, and all the other nitty-gritty things discussed above.

At the end of the day, do what is best for you, your LLC, or your LLC turned corporation, by following the recommendations in this chapter.

CHAPTER SIX

ACCOUNTING FOR YOUR LLC

You may want to do your own bookkeeping or accounting, but you should consult a professional. It is not absolutely necessary, but a professional bookkeeper, auditor, or accountant worth their salt, will structure your LLC in the most effective way possible.

There are so many starter bookkeeping instruction manuals out there, and if your business is relatively simple, such as my former salt trading LLC, then there is no reason why you can't do your own books.

Having said that, I used an accountant as I was a bit unsure of my own ability and thought it best to use an expert. You can get started on your own but appoint a professional according to the growth of your business.

Ask yourself whether you want to pay more tax or less tax, and let your answer influence your decision in this regard. I kind of sway between doing it myself and appointing someone. When I am favoring doing it myself, I flick through my old high school accounting textbook, and it usually changes my mind, but as I have said so many times, it is a personal choice.

'General ledger' is one of the buzz phrases when it comes to accounting, auditing, and bookkeeping, so let me explain it in greater detail.

What is a General Ledger and What Does it Record?

A general ledger is used to comprehensively record all financial transactions of a business, be it a sole proprietorship, corporation, or LLC. Even if you have decided to appoint a professional, it is still important to understand the importance of a general ledger, and to get a basic idea of how it is utilized.

Let's look at some general ledger transactions.

LLC Investment Assets

These don't have to be actual tangible assets, they could be stocks, shares, NFT's, or cryptocurrency. Real estate is generally seen as a low-risk asset, and your LLC might start out small by buying an office to work from and expand its property portfolio from there.

Every amount spent in pursuit of asset investment must be recorded and backed up with the necessary sale or transfer documentation.

Equipment

Your LLC may need office equipment, let's say a large printer, which can be bought or leased. It is arguably better to lease in this situation, as breakdowns or other issues are often attended to as part of the monthly payments. Whatever the nature of the transaction, the amount must be recorded, and any relevant invoices, payment receipts, written agreements, and everything to do with that transaction or those transactions must be kept.

Income and Expenditure

This is simple, kind of. Any money that comes into your LLC and any money that leaves your LLC should be recorded in a general ledger. Credit lines to customers must match up to invoices and so must your business credit, be it from suppliers or outside credit providers.

The same applies to cash received or paid, even though actual cash in hand will become obsolete, it can't be ignored, and must be recorded in the general ledger.

At the end of the day, you don't want the IRS to discover that your accounting system is up the pole, so to speak. Also, keeping accurate records will assist tremendously if your LLC is audited. You don't want to spend days searching for receipts, invoices, statements, credit slips, and other documents that match the transactions in the general ledger.

You need to be diligent from step one.

Best Method of Taxation

Whilst it is important to keep the IRS happy, it is also important to minimize your tax, *within* the law. Please don't try and practice 'accounting gymnastics' and hide income from the tax man. You will regret it at a later stage when it catches up with you! Many successful businesspeople have undone themselves and ended up in jail by succumbing to this temptation.

Your options in terms of taxation are to be taxed as a partnership, sole proprietorship, or corporation.

Partnership

If you wish for your LLC to be taxed as a partnership, you should complete a form called '1065.' It can be found on the IRS website and requires a lot of information, so it can be very time consuming.

This is not something you want to risk messing up, so a tax expert should be appointed. There are sections about legal compliance and Act numbers, which a tax person will know backwards, so even if you need to shell out some money, it is a worthwhile investment in the long run. You could also get a tax lawyer to assist you.

Sole Proprietorship

The form required for taxation as a sole proprietor is called a '1040,' also referred to as a 'Schedule C' form. It requires income and expenditure declarations, and whilst it isn't terribly long, I would recommend a tax expert just like with a partnership.

This form can also be obtained from the IRS website.

Corporation

Corporation tax requirements are put forward in a form from the IRS, called a '1120-S,' which can also be found on the IRS website. The form is a bit shorter than the others, but also a bit more complicated, so the same moral of the same story applies, use a professional for assistance.

Choosing the Best Accounting System

The best accounting system for you will depend on the size of your business, and it can be said that registering for tax and complying with all the legislation is a more arduous task than the actual bookkeeping.

Easy right? Money in less money out equals taxable profit... but not quite!

Accrual Basis Accounting

This refers to accounting for transactions that may not have left your account or come into your account. Accrual basis accounting serves businesses that have accounts with suppliers and service providers, and that grants credit to customers.

Let's say your business buys and sells swimming pool equipment, there is a likelihood that you will pay every 30 days. For instance, all your orders in June, you will pay for at the end of July, but the money is recorded as if it has left the business account.

The same applies to your customers, who have 30-day accounts with your business, so although the money is expected in a month's time, it is recorded as having been already received.

Cash Basis Accounting

The system of recording money in and out is the same, but the transactions are recorded at the time that the money comes in and goes out.

I mentioned my LLC earlier, where I bought and sold commodities, and although I did have and provided the accounts, I still recorded transactions on a cash basis. To me, and for my business purposes, I find cash accounting easier to manage, and I love the saying, "Cash is King."

Which Method Do You Use

The latter, cash basis accounting, is favored by freelancers and 'one-man' bands as it is more straightforward. Not to say that multiple member LLCs and other entities must choose cash basis accounting, but if simple is what you are after, then I would recommend cash records.

Accrual based accounting suits bigger businesses where there are several transactions every day, so working from a 30-day credit statement from customers is much easier than trawling through a plethora of transactions. The same would be the case with 30 day credit from suppliers.

Look into the nitty gritty a bit more with professional advice before you come to a decision.

How to Set Up Your Bookkeeping System

Whether you have decided on accrual basis accounting or cash basis accounting, you will have to set up a bookkeeping system, of which there are several. I will take you through the three most relevant and commonly used systems to allow you to make an informed decision.

Do It Yourself Bookkeeping

This is more suited to small businesses, and you can simply use an excel spreadsheet to track income and expenses. You also have the option of using a cloud-based system of bookkeeping, which are very reasonably priced. My personal recommendations would be SagePay or Quickbooks, as they are very user friendly, and back system support is very good.

You have to be very disciplined in this case, you can't leave the books for weeks and tell yourself that you will attend to them at a later stage. When you reach that later stage, you will have created so much extra work for yourself, and the possibility of big confusion.

Outsourced Bookkeeping

You don't want to appoint a huge accounting firm that charges an arm and a leg, so an actual bookkeeper would be fine. There are quite a few bookkeepers that do freelance work after they retire, so ask around and get referrals before choosing someone for the position.

Also, you need to check their work, and even though your bookkeeper should be an expert, mistakes can be made. I have found, through experience, that I have better relationships with bookkeepers, well more accountants, when they send me work to run my eyes over and approve, alternatively raise concerns.

In-House Bookkeeping

This will become necessary if you are spending too much time on the bookkeeping side yourself, instead of focusing on making money, or if your outsourced bookkeeper becomes out of their depth. It will be the costliest method but will probably be justified in these circumstances.

Make sure you get the right person, just in the earlier case of the right manager.

How to Keep Track of Your Expenses

Your expenses are obviously recorded no matter what bookkeeping system you choose, and please remember that every entry into your books needs to be backed up by the necessary documentation.

If you have a business meeting over lunch, you need to keep a copy of the receipt. The same applies to company credit card purchases, such as flights to attend a conference. Monthly accounts from service providers, such as your electricity and water bill or office phone statement, must also be kept. You get the idea.

Develop a good filing system and make sure you are aware of the legislation in the state(s) where your business is registered. By law, you have to keep certain records for X number of years, usually between three and ten years, but it is not a bad idea to hang onto your records indefinitely.

There are companies that provide file storage facilities, but they come with a cost, and the risk of your business information being accessible to others is high (hypothetically).

Chapter Summary

Accounting is very important for tax purposes, record keeping, and forecasting. You can, of course, do it yourself, but may prefer to use an expert. Essentially you need to keep and maintain a general ledger, to record investment or equipment purchases, income and expenses, and any miscellaneous transactions that impact your business.

You need to decide on your tax system, and complete the correct IRS forms, whether you want to be taxed as a partnership, sole proprietorship, or corporation.

Next, you need to assess whether you use the accrual or cash system of bookkeeping. Accrual usually works best with accounts, and I gave the 30-day example. Income and expenditure is recorded before it leaves or arrives in your account, whereas the cash system details cash out when it leaves, and cash in when it arrives.

You may want to keep your books yourself, on a spreadsheet, or using cloud-based software, otherwise outsource or hire an in-house bookkeeper. When making the decision, consider that your primary role should be making the business successful.

Keeping records of expenses is important, and backup documents, such as receipts or credit card statements, must be filed and kept for a certain period, depending on which state(s) your LLC is registered in.

All of this is very important, and if done correctly, will save you heaps of time if you are audited by the IRS, or are required to produce records for any other reason.

Chapter Seven

FILING TAXES AS AN LLC

Tax season—nobody's favorite—is very necessary. Well, maybe a favorite of the accountants and bookkeepers. There is a huge honesty element here, and I would strongly advise you not to hide anything from the IRS, not even once. You need to be able to sleep at night, knowing that you are compliant.

Consider that taxation depends on the number of members of your LLC. As I have stated previously, your LLC can be taxed as a corporation, which may save you money when it comes to IRS payments. LLC's can certainly have non-taxable deductions, but it is vital that you hit the filing deadlines to avoid penalties.

So, here is some information on what needs to be done to be compliant. Don't forget that there are different challenges in terms of different business structures, but they should be expected and anticipated.

Requirements for Single Member LLC's

A sole proprietorship and a single member LLC are treated in exactly the same way by the IRS. They are basically identical, except, obviously, the LLC provides that personal protection. Either way, the IRS requires that you file a personal tax return. See the links in the previous chapter, where you can get the necessary forms, from the IRS website. There is an extra step for a single member LLC, and that is filing the Schedule C, profit or loss report for the business.

Pretty straightforward; revenue, less business expenditure, equals profit or loss (hopefully profit). Revenue is simpler, being whatever money comes in, whether you sell a product or sell your time. Expenditure is anything from office rental, telephone costs, fuel for business related travel, purchasing products, to wages for temps, or printer repairs. Basically, any necessary costs of running your business. The end figure of this calculation is added to your personal tax filings.

Requirements for Multiple Member LLC's

Whether your LLC has two or ten members, or any amount from two upwards, it is seen as a partnership by the IRS. To put it in simple terms, members are taxed on their personal profits, which will usually correspond with the amount invested by said members.

On the form 1065, being the US Return of Partnership Income, the LLC is required to submit its profit and loss statement, along with a declaration of deductible expenses. Next, your balance sheet shows all financial information from beginning to end of the tax year, and this is where accurate record keeping is vital.

Another form, just a one-pager, is needed; Schedule K-1, part of the 1065. This lays out the different percentage shares of the members, which allows the IRS to examine personal profits.

Schedule E records the profits and losses of each individual member of the LCC.

All the forms should be filed together to show that tax is being taken seriously, but also because it provides for less administration. You always want to be seen as timeous and compliant by the IRS.

C-Corp Versus S-Corp

As you should know by now, an LLC can choose to be taxed as a corporation, which provides for a different framework. There are various requirements, some onerous, some not so much.

C-Corp

The first document that must be filed, if you want to create a C-Corp is Form 8832, which is your Entity Classification Election document. The requirements to qualify, or operate, if you like, as a C-Corp are to establish a board of directors, issue shares to investors, and designate positions within the C-Corp, such as shareholders, officers, employees, etc.

There must be an annual meeting of shareholders, where detailed minutes are taken and recorded electronically. To be fair, this should be done at every single meeting no matter what the topics on the agenda are, but I guess you could say that the annual meeting holds the most importance.

Your LLC files its own tax return and so does each member. This creates a double taxation, which is the most common reason for straying away from being taxed as a C-Corp.

See the forms on the IRS website.

S-Corp

There are several requirements to qualify your LLC as an S-Corp, but they are not complicated; however, you must follow them exactly and thoroughly. Making a checklist, and ticking off things as you complete them, is a useful strategy.

Be a domestic corporation

You must only do business in the state in which the LLC is registered (remember domestic and foreign LLC classification from prior chapters).

Have 100 or less shareholders

A bit of an arbitrary one, but if you are just starting up an LLC, it is highly unlikely that your members will exceed 100. Shareholders can consist of individuals, trusts and estates, but not partnerships, corporations, or non-domestic businesses.

Be Eligible to Operate as an S-Corp

Insurance companies and banks cannot operate as an S-corp. There are other institutions that are ineligible, and by consulting a tax expert, you can establish which institutions do and don't qualify.

Have Only One Class of Stock

This way, ownership rights are standardized, which provides for more control. The IRS allows an S-Corp to pass income, expenditure, and anything similar in respect of financials through the shareholders, for federal tax.

The Schedule E and Schedule K-1, as discussed earlier must also be filed with the IRS, for both sets of corporations. Follow the link that I provided earlier.

Estimated Tax, What and Why?

Corporations are required to pay estimated tax on a quarterly basis. Although not the official term, this type of tax is also called provisional tax. Personally, I don't like this method because if you are inaccurate in your estimations, you may owe the IRS more than you think. Having said that, there are measures and steps to follow, so that you can be as accurate as possible in your estimates. There are also steep penalties for late filing, but you should never file late in any case, it's akin to throwing away money.

Remember that if you are an employee, your taxes are automatically withheld from your salary, so as an owner, member, shareholder, etc., you are said to be, or at least treated as being, self-employed. This means that accurately calculating taxes that would ordinarily be withheld, is not an exact science, hence the need to estimate.

I could sum it up by saying that as an employee, your exact tax liability is easy to calculate, and your monthly deductions are invariable, with the possible exception of commission-based income. Being self-employed, or regarded as, means that your income, profits, and losses are variable, and change often, depending on several factors.

Essentially, you need to give the IRS an accurate, let's call it projected, idea of what you earn, and the tax on that amount. As your business grows, you will learn how to be more accurate with your estimations because you develop data that you can call on to aim towards that accuracy.

If it is your very first year of trading, accurate estimates are challenging, but as your business continues you gain estimating experience, to put it very simply. In the beginning, it is best to use a tax expert, and depending on the business variables as you grow, you may be able to file estimated tax on your own. Expert first though!

How to Calculate Estimated Tax

You will need to combine your business income with any other income, and also record any tax withholding, deductions, and credits to get to a position which is as accurate as possible.

Remember to record *all* sources of income, and all applicable expenses, to arrive at your estimation. This would include any passive income from business investments. You can project this by looking at previous years trading spreadsheets and analyzing your likely income, or based on future projections, in cases where you have secured significant contracts.

It can be useful to separate income and expenses into two categories, being fixed and variable.

Fixed Income

An employee has a fixed monthly income, but a business, as a whole, can enjoy certain fixed income sources, too. Perhaps you have customers who pay a monthly retainer fee for your service, alternatively your business may hold rental investments, and that income amount does not change except upon renewal of lease, but that is only once a year, generally.

Variable Income

This is pretty much sales. Your turnover won't be the same every month, and there are a host of different reasons, but simply put, sales vary. There are often certain times of the year that are busier than others, so you should expect ups and downs in turnover.

Remember that consultants sell their time, along with many other professions, so when I say 'sales' I don't only mean tangible selling only.

Fixed Expenses

Office rental, employee salaries, union fees, Wi-Fi costs, insurance, and any other expenses that have an exact amount that doesn't change from month to month. These are not estimates, but form part of the bigger estimate picture.

These expenses are easier to keep tabs on because they don't change, so there is a lot less reconciliation of invoices and statements, with money received, or paid out.

Variable Expenses

The value of these expenses' changes, and some may be more intermittent than others. These may be, cost of stock, office repair, printer servicing, bank fees, and any other expenses that vary from one to another and in frequency.

The Actual Calculation

Work out your fixed income, then average out your variable income, and arrive at an amount, which you will call total income.

Work out fixed expenses, then average out variable expenses, and you get your total expenses, just as you did with income.

Subtract your two totals, and you have your taxable income.

This is a very simplified explanation, but it will give you a clear basis and framework from which a tax expert can assist, if you decide that you need one.

Personal Tax Component

You are compelled to include your personal income, credits, exemptions, deductions, and withholding of federal taxes, when you file your personal return.

You must be aware of social security taxes, or medical cover/care protection taxes as well. These form part of your self-employment tax, and cannot be ignored or left out.

There are both advantages and disadvantages.

Social Security Taxes

If your combined income ranges from $25,000 to $34000, up to 50% of your social security benefit will be taxed, more than $34,000 and you will be taxed on around 85% of your social security benefits.

You can obtain a social security benefit statement from the IRS, which indicates your benefits over the previous year. This must be used when you submit your federal tax return, and you will be able to ascertain whether you will be taxed, and at what percentage you will be taxed.

Medical Care Taxation

Certain medical expenses are tax exempt.

The following is taken directly from the IRS website, and succinctly explains the situation, "Medical care expenses include payments for the diagnosis, cure, mitigation, treatment, or prevention of disease, or payments for treatments affecting any structure or function of the body."

There is a long list of specific tax-deductible medical expenses on the said IRS website.

You can only deduct medical expenses if they exceed 7.5% of your adjusted gross income, so keep that in mind when you itemize your deductions in the relevant section of the form.

Chapter Summary

Taxation depends on a few factors. Single member LLCs are taxed on the difference between revenue and expenses, as is a sole proprietorship.

Multiple member LLCs require a profit and loss statement and an itemized set of deductible expenses in order to comply with IRS regulations.

You have the choice of a C-Corp or an S-corp. For the former, there has to be a board of directors, appointed shareholders, formal issuing of shares, and defining of business positions. In these instances, the LLC files and the members also file in their personal capacity. S-corps have different requirements, such as domestic domicile, and a 100-member limit on shareholders, amongst others.

Using fixed and variable income and expenses, you can produce an estimate of your taxes. Social Security and Medicare taxes must be considered and depending on turnover factors and specific non-taxable medical expenses, you will be able to arrive at figures, as to your tax benefits.

If you follow the above, with help from professionals if needed, you can rest easy that the IRS is happy.

Just a quick bit of advice. I often skip ahead when reading a document, assuming that I have full knowledge, and I am most often incorrect. Don't do that! Follow the links that pertain to your business situation and read *and* understand the requirements as thoroughly as possible.

CHAPTER EIGHT

DISSOLVING AN LLC

T here are several reasons for dissolving an LLC, and this is where limiting your liability comes into play. Not in every case, but you should have peace of mind, that you are protected in a situation where dissolution is forced due to circumstance.

When Should You Dissolve Your LLC?

The short answer is that you should dissolve your LLC when the purpose of that LLC has been completed or if continuing to operate your LLC is no longer financially viable. These are the reasons why you created an LLC in the first place.

If the Purpose for Creating the LLC Has Been Fulfilled/Come to an End

This is pretty straightforward, your LLC may have been formed with an expiration date, generally depending on the occurrence of a likely future event. This doesn't mean that the business has to stop operating when that point is reached. You may have a specific plan and want to restructure, for instance.

The purpose of the LLC may be to tender for a supply contract, that is a once off, for say 12 months. When the contract has come to an end, and your LLC has been compliant in every regard, especially tax, you can then dissolve it. This will be recorded in the beginning, of course.

If Financial Viability No Longer Exists

If your LLC is continually making losses and you have taken every measure that you can in order to mitigate the situation but with no success, then you are compelled to dissolve the LLC.

Some measures could be making employees redundant, which is always terrible, and something that should only be done in extreme circumstances. Otherwise, you can look at payment arrangements with overdue creditors or extension of payment deadlines. An investor may help, but if your LLC is really struggling, the likelihood of that is limited.

Unfortunately, many businesses face closure, and often through outside influences; the most obvious example being Covid-19. You don't ever want your LLC to be in such a position, but at least you have that personal protection.

Types of Dissolution

I mentioned financial viability, and if you are for all intents and purposes a broke LLC, you are said to be bankrupt. You can voluntarily dissolve your LLC, but you may encounter dissolution at the hands of creditors, which is then classified as involuntary.

Let's say your LLC has credit with a bank, and it also owes your supplier a large sum of money. Either one of these creditors can apply to have your LLC dissolved, in the hope that they will get at least some of what they are owed through the sale of LLC assets and seizure of cash.

Voluntary Dissolution

This does not only apply to lack of financial viability, but it does apply in cases where the purpose of the LLC has come to an end. Let's have a look at the steps to follow.

You Have to Vote to Dissolve the LLC

Your operating agreement should provide details as to dissolution, but if it doesn't, then the members will have to vote to decide if the purpose for creating the LLC has ended. It may be the death of a shareholder, or as I mentioned previously, the end of a once off contract.

These events are referred to as dissolution triggers, and whether specified or not, and whether a vote is required or not, the decision to dissolve the LLC must be recorded and filed with the LLC's records.

Financial viability may require a vote, but if the situation is so dire, all members should easily agree to dissolve the LLC for personal protection.

Filing Your Final Tax Return

If you still owe the IRS money, or are not up to date with your returns, then you will have to prepare and submit your final return, and pay whatever tax is required or claim tax refunds payable to your LLC.

Once this process is completed, your LLC will be compliant and will be issued with some form of compliance certificate or letter of compliance, which differ from state to state. You do have to indicate on your return that it is your final one, and that the reason is dissolution of your LLC.

Obviously, you have to file the returns associated with your choice of taxation, and that may include federal tax returns, as well as employment tax returns, without which you will not be compliant.

Filing an Article of Dissolution

This is an official request for the state to allow dissolution of your LLC. A standard form to assist you can be found on the Secretary of State website.

The form requires business information, as well as details of the members and recordable asset distribution. Perhaps you had to sell assets to settle debts. Your liabilities must also be specified. Look at it as a short story of your LLC's position at the time, how you arrived at that position, followed by a request for your certificate of dissolution.

You will have to pay a small fee and file the certificate with your business records. You should remember me saying earlier that records have to be kept for certain amounts of time. This applies even in cases of dissolution.

Settling Outstanding Debts

This may be difficult, especially if you are in a financial situation where further business operations are not viable.

Even if not specifically required, you should notify your creditors that you would like to settle their accounts, and request that they put in claims for you to ascertain final figures.

The same applies if you can only partly pay or cannot pay at all. You will have to notify them of your inability to pay and request that they put in claims against your LLC.

Procedures differ depending on your state, and you may have to publish a notice calling on your creditors to submit claims, or pin notices up at the court which has jurisdiction.

The general idea is to use all money and assets owned by the business to pay, or at least partially pay, creditors.

Sale or Distribution of Assets

If you are fortunate enough to have assets remaining after settling all your LLC's debt, those assets will be sold and the proceeds distributed amongst the members, alternatively the physical assets are distributed.

The distribution process, and what may be distributed can be obtained from your operating agreement, or according to state law.

Complete Other Winding Down Processes

You will have to notify customers, suppliers, service providers, and employees of the dissolution. This should all be in writing, or you can call meetings with the above entities or people, then follow up with written confirmation.

Closing Bank Accounts

The last task is to close your business bank account(s) and "retire" both your federal and state taxation identification number.

And just like that, your LLC has been dissolved, and any liability of that LLC, does not pass on to you, and/or other members.

Involuntary Dissolution

This may be the result if your LLC becomes bankrupt, if shareholders cannot agree on dissolution, if there is evidence of fraud, or if the LLC does not comply with tax and legal requirements.

The court will enforce dissolution in cases like this, but more specifically, creditors will kick off dissolution procedures in the hope that the LLC has enough money and assets to settle their claims.

Once the creditors are settled, or partially settled from actual money and money raised by sale of assets, the members are exempt from personal liability relating to outstanding amounts owed to creditors.

The same process of notifying customers, creditors, suppliers, etc., applies, although the court is more involved, meaning that notices are kind of done for your LLC.

Just like voluntary dissolution, tax has to be up to date, and the process ends with a certificate of dissolution, or a letter to the same effect, after the state is satisfied that your LLC has complied with all requirements.

From that point, no member is liable in any capacity for outstanding business debts, but do not forget about…

The Exception, Personal Surety

Avoid signing personal surety because that negates the whole point of limited liability. If you do sign personal surety, and the LLC owes the bank a substantial amount, you, as the surety, become liable as a natural person.

Unfortunately, some banks and financiers will not give credit to an LLC if nobody is prepared to stand personal surety, but 'private' investors may not enforce the same requirement.

Personal suretyship can be seen as a convention to limit the liability of credit providers, so try your best not to be put in a position where a deal won't go through without some form of surety.

Chapter Summary

When an LLC has completed the purpose for which it was created, you can voluntarily dissolve the LLC by sole decision if you are the only member, or via a vote if you are part of a multiple member LLC.

You will have to file your final tax return, as well as your articles of dissolution (the story of the business, and why its purpose has been completed).

The LLC's debts must be settled, and this may involve selling assets. It may be the case that the sale of assets and liquid cash in the business bank account don't raise enough to pay off all creditors, in which case, when dissolution is complete, those creditors cannot come after your personal assets.

In an involuntary dissolution, your creditors may apply for dissolution, but thereafter the process is the same and your personal assets are still protected.

You also need to wind everything down by informing your customers and employees through due process.

Finally, you will need to terminate contracts with service providers and close the business bank account(s).

A word of warning, *never* sign as a personal surety because it negates the limitation of your liability.

CONCLUSION

I hope by this point you have absorbed and understood the key factors surrounding LLCs, and everything thereto related. I also hope you have enjoyed the read and feel confident about making business decisions, in terms of LLCs, that will be beneficial and prosperous. So, I would like to conclude with a summary and leave you inspired to pursue your business goals!

Limiting your personal liability, which is essentially separating it from your business liability, gives you that much needed peace of mind. If your LLC runs into financial trouble, your personal assets, whatever they may be, are safe. This is a major advantage of LLCs, and arguably the main reason for their development.

Other major advantages are the ability to structure your entity in an effective tax manner. The fact that you are taxed as an individual, whether you operate as a single or multiple member LLC, is a certain advantage.

For me, the simpler the better, and setting up LLC's does not require endless meetings, long reams of paper, shareholders resolutions, and business delaying processes. Your major disadvantage can be cost, but that is largely dependent on which state your LLC is domiciled in.

The next consideration is single or multiple member LLC's. I like the fact that the former allows complete control as I am not a fan of making decisions as part of a group, but having said that, if you have the right set of members, joint decision making shouldn't become a problem. The fact is that LLC's, are in general, simple entities that can be very effective, in all areas.

Corporations have to be considered, and LLC's can be taxed as corporations. Remember that corporations have shareholders and percentage ownership is determined by percentage shareholding. Although corporations are subject to a much more stringent set of regulations, outside investment is generally obtainable, which can be vital to new businesses.

If you do favor operating as an LLC, you will need to consider whether your LLC will be member managed, or manager managed. If it is new, and you are the only member, you may want to do everything yourself, to limit costs. Even if your LLC has multiple members, you can collectively choose the member management option. Certain businesses require a manager, and although a manager comes with a cost, you, as a single member or as part of a multiple member LLC, can decide on the financial viability. If you put too much on your plate, you will be spread too thin, so the cost of a manager would be justified. Then you and/or your partners can focus on making the business succeed.

Another major decision is whether you want to register your LLC as domestic or foreign. The former means that the LLC is domiciled in one state (domestic state), and the latter refers to an LLC that is also registered in a foreign state. If you only do business in one state then there may be no reason to register your LLC as foreign, but a business, such as a retail chain that has shops in several states, must be registered as foreign. Don't forget that the LLC will always be domestic in one state.

If you require a business license to practice your profession, such as a doctor or an accountant, you will have to form a Professional Limited Liability Company, so in such a case, decision made.

A lessor favored option is a Series LLC, which has a parent LLC, that is a member of another LLC, along with individuals, as members. These types of LLC's are suited to multiple opportunity businesses, such as real estate ownership. Liability is limited on the behalf of individual members, but also as the member-LLC.

Naming your LLC is important, and you must consider your industry, target market, and credibility establishment, through your name.

You will need to prepare and file the articles of association with the correct state authority. You can appoint an agent to assist and to receive legal and/or financial documentation; however, you can be your own agent. A lawyer can be effective, but is not a stipulation, and a tax expert can be used to guide you along. These two people can help you with business credit information and LLC compliance to keep your LLC alive.

Be careful of registering the wrong entity or making bad tax decisions. For instance, if your annual profit is $80,000 or more, your LLC must be taxed as an S-Corp for tax efficiency.

Make sure you choose the correct state, and that you comply with regulations, even those that may sound frivolous, such as having 'LLC' suffixed to your business name.

Don't take shortcuts, always follow the correct processes, after all, something very avoidable, like letting your license lapse, could kill your business. Think carefully about future possibilities or occurrences, such as a deadlocked vote, in trying to arrive at a business decision. These types of things must be recorded in your operating agreement, with other, more obvious provisions, such as not mixing personal and business funds. Keep your operating agreement up to date, as this is the basis for dispute resolution, as the 'rules' are in black and white.

You may want to convert an existing business into an LLC, whether it be an already created LLC and LLC group, or more commonly, a sole proprietorship. First, do your homework, perhaps in consultation with a lawyer or accountant. You don't want to be in a position where asset sale/transfer leaves you with a giant gains tax bill.

If you are satisfied that you are doing the right thing for your business, then you will need to comply with the specified regulations, like filling in the correct forms, drafting the required agreements, opening a new business banking account, etc.

Accounting is vital, and you must keep a general ledger that records every single transaction, from investment assets purchase or sale to equipment costs and income and expenditure, plus any other relevant transaction.

Look into taxation as a partnership, sole-proprietorship, or corporation, and make a call as to which is compatible with your business.

Decide if you want to use accrual-based bookkeeping, where transactions are recorded as if they have been executed, even if payment of an account is only due at month-end. Your other option is cash-based bookkeeping, where transactions are recorded as and when they happen. Another consideration is whether you will do the books yourself, outsource, or employ someone in a permanent position. This is very individual, and factors may be ability, time, and cost.

When filing taxes, you must remember that single member LLCs are taxed in the same way as sole proprietorships and multiple member LLCs are taxed on profits in line with percentage shareholding.

If you elect to be taxed as a C-Corp, take note of the fact that a board is required, shares must be officially issued, and meetings are commonplace in decision making. In C-corp taxation the LLC files, and so do its members.

In an S-Corp, there are different regulations, for instance, as an LLC, you cannot have more than 100 members and be taxed as an S-corp. With S-Corp taxation, income, expenditure, and other transactions are passed through the shareholders for federal tax.

These systems use quarterly estimated tax, and the idea is to use all fixed and variable income and expenses, along with other tax impacting transactions, as predictors of future tax. Don't forget the possible benefits of social security benefits and non-taxable Medicare expenses. You want to do everything you can (legally) to pay as little tax as possible.

Your LLC may have been set up for a single purpose, such as fulfilling one contract. When that purpose is complete, the LLC must be dissolved. Alternatively, if setting up your LLC was for continued business, and you find that it falls into financially non-viable waters, you will have to dissolve.

Voluntary dissolution is decided upon via a vote, unless you are the only LLC member, but either way, when the decision is made, you will need to prepare to submit your final tax return, along with your articles of dissolution, which basically tell the story of the business and its life span.

You need to settle debts, to suppliers, service providers, banks, financiers, etc., and to do that you will be required to use money remaining in the business, along with sale of assets. Now, if your liquid money and asset value cannot service your debt, one of your creditors may launch a dissolution application, which then makes the dissolution involuntary.

This is where your personal liability is limited. If you sell everything and pay what you can, then no entity can come after you personally in any way, which is arguably the most important reason for forming an LLC. Do not compromise your personal liability by signing a suretyship. If you go against this advice, then the primary reason for forming your LLC is made redundant as you will no longer have personal protection.

The laws around LLC's were enacted specifically, so use them to your advantage, that is what they are there for!

I will leave you with a tip, and every reader would have heard it before, but it is important. Don't let anyone tell you that your business will fail, that you are crazy to start a particular business, or that you are not suited to business.

If it fails, so what? You can pick yourself up and start again, after all, many billionaires have failed dozens of times before tasting success.

EPILOGUE

What follows is a list that should guide you through the process of setting up your LLC. My advice would be to read the steps and refer to the body of this book if you need clarity on any aspects. The below list is not exhaustive, so there may be points that don't apply to your business specifically, but the majority of the list deals with the administrative requirements, along with some useful tips.

1. Decide whether you want to be the sole-member, or whether you want to have another or multiple members.

2. Once you have made that decision, establish whether you want to hire a manager.

3. If you are a licensed member of a profession, such as a doctor or accountant, ensure that such licenses are up to date.

4. Get professional tax advice before choosing to register a domestic LLC or a foreign LLC. This will save you money.

5. Appoint your agent and go through the administrative processes in Chapter Three. Get all the paperwork done, double check, and submit.

6. When your LLC is registered, open a business bank account. There are many options, specific to LLC's. My three recommendations would be Bluevine, Lily, and US Bank. Take a look at their websites, write your questions down, make contact, and when you are fully informed, make your choice.

7. Look into business credit. A good starting point is to look at the U.S. Small Business Administration website. They have a tool called, 'lender match' and will pair you up with the financial institution that best suits your LLC.

8. Chapter Six will help you to understand what a general ledger is, but you need to make an informed decision as to your accounting system. Sage Pay or Quickbooks are user friendly, and will allow you to do your own accounting, but outsourcing or an in-house accountant must be considered.

9. Tax compliance is very important, so relying on a professional is a good idea. There are several forms to fill in and you can get them from the USA Corporate Services Inc. website, alternative from the IRS website or at your local IRS office.

10. Develop a filing system before you start operating your LLC. Print out any and all forms, including your operating agreements, minutes of meetings, tax compliance notices, credit agreements, etc. This will prevent any confusion or disagreement in the future. In addition to that, LLC's and other entities are required by law to keep records for certain periods. This differs from state to state, so make sure you check.

11. Commence business… You know what to do here, as you are the owner, or co-owner. So run your LLC as best possible, and I hope that you succeed in whatever sphere or niche your

business fits into. There will be hard days and tough moments. You will need to work hard, but the rewards will come. Be patient!

12. In the future you may need to dissolve your LLC, either because it has fulfilled its purpose or because it is no longer economically viable. Regarding the latter, you are protected as an individual from personal liability, which is one of the reasons that you formed your LLC in the beginning.

13. Chapter Eight deals with dissolution, and if you do reach such a point, your best bet is to use a lawyer or accountant to assist in selling assets, paying off debts, filing the LLC's last tax return, closing the LLC bank accounts, and doing all else required to complete the dissolution process.

14. Avoid, as far as reasonably possible, signing as personal surety for any debt that may arise out of the day-to-day operation of the LLC. If you do sign surety, you are 'un-limiting' your liability. LLCs were designed to give you that personal protection, and as is the case, limiting that personal liability is the point. Please do your best to remember that it is very important.

REFERENCES

Crail, C. Haskins, J. Watts, R. (2022, July 8). *What is a Limited Liability Company (LLC)?* Definition, Pro's and Con's. <u>What Is An LLC? Definition, Pros & Cons – Forbes Advisor</u>

UpCounsel Technologies, various authors (2022, month and date unknown). *Explain LLC:* Everything You Need to Know. <u>Explain LLC: Everything You Need to Know (upcounsel.com)</u>

Haskins, J. (2022, May 2). *LLC vs Corporation:* Which One is Right for Me? <u>LLC vs. Corporation: Which One is Right for Me? | LegalZoom</u>

Silver, C. Attkinson, A. Woosley, B. Kagan, J. Chaturvedi, V. Wrenn, S. Alpert, C. Halton, C. Feldman, J. Laidley, C. Williams, W. (2021, July 30). What is the History of Corporations in America? <u>https://www.investopedia.com/ask/answers/041515/what-history-corporations-america.asp#:~:text=The%20first%20American%20corporations%20were,d evelopment%20like%20the%20United%20States</u>.

History.com, editors, various. (2010, April 9). *John D. Rockefeller.* <u>https://www.history.com/topics/early-20th-century-us/john-d-rockefeller</u>

History.com, editors, various. (2009, November 9). *Andrew Carnegie.* <u>https://www.history.com/topics/19th-century/andrew-carnegie</u>

Akalp, N. (2021, August 10). *LLC.* <u>Which LLC Is Right for Me? (corpnet.com)</u>

Berry-Johnson, J. (2022, January 3). *Corporation*: What is it and How to Form One? https://www.investopedia.com/terms/c/corporation.asp

Watts, R. Haskins, J. (2022, September 4). *How to Set Up an LLC in 7 Steps. How To Set Up An LLC In 7 Steps – Forbes Advisor*

Sember, B. (2022, July 28). *Which State Should You File Your LLC in?* Which State Should You File Your LLC In? | LegalZoom

Jefferson, R. (2020, August 25). *4 Common Mistakes That People Make When Running an LLC.* 4 Common Mistakes People Make When Running An LLC – Lawyers Rock

Wong, B. (2022, May 2). *Should You Convert Your Corporation to an LLC?* Should You Convert Your Corporation to an LLC? | LegalZoom

Organ, C. Main, K. (2022, August 18). How to Change a Sole Proprietorship to an LLC in 6 Steps. https://www.forbes.com/advisor/business/how-change-sole-proprietorship-to-llc/

Research Team, Knowledge Hub. (2022, April 26). *Everything You Need to Know About Accounting for an LLC.* Everything You Need to Know About Accounting for an LLC (generisonline.com)

Murphy, K. (2022, August 15). *Small Business Accounting:* How to Set Up and Manage Your Books. Small Business Accounting 101: Basics, Set Up, Software (2022) (shopify.co.uk)

Unknown Author. (2019, March 28). *Small Business Accounting 101*: A Ten Step Guide for Financial Success. Small Business Accounting 101 | a 10-Step Guide for Financial Success (freshbooks.com)

Martins, A. (2022, August 12). *Which LLC Taxes Must Your Business File. LLC Tax Guide - businessnewsdaily.com*

Haskin, J. (2022, May 2). *6 Steps to Filing Corporation Taxes. https://www.legalzoom.com/articles/6-steps-to-filing-corporation-taxes.*

Murray, J. (2022, September 11). *How do I Calculate Estimated Taxes for my Business?* How Do I Calculate Estimated Taxes for My Business? (thebalancemoney.com)

Watts, R. Haskin, J (2022, July 8). *How to Effectively Dissolve an LLC.* *How To Dissolve An LLC – Forbes Advisor*

S-CORP BEGINNER'S GUIDE (UPDATED EDITION)

The Most Complete and Easy-to-Follow Handbook on How to Manage Your S-Corporation

Steven Carlson

INTRODUCTION

Your business goals will define the type of entity that you create in order to start trading effectively. There are certain factors that are important to consider, for instance, legal protection, operations, and tax management. This book addresses these factors, as well as all others relevant to S-Corporations (S-Corp).

An S-Corp draws similarities with other structures of corporations in terms of Subchapter S of Chapter One of the Internal Revenue Code. The laws codified therein are enforced by the Internal Revenue Service (IRS). As per the IRS definition, an S-Corp is as follows, directly quoted (Home: Internal Revenue Service):

"Any business that chooses to pass corporate income, losses, deductions, and credits, through shareholders for federal tax purposes, with the benefit of limited liability, and relief from double taxation."

The above may raise some questions, and to answer such questions, I will break down the definition and explain the different parts. Remember that each type of entity, like each type of business, has its advantages and disadvantages. The idea is to objectively assess the said business vehicle and to do that. I am going to go through the pros and cons of S-Corps in detail.

It is also necessary to understand sole proprietorships. The business owner is the only person involved, and that means that he or she IS the business. I will explain the ramifications of not having the limited liability that other entities have. I will then move on to partnerships, explore what types of businesses can benefit the most from partnerships, and discuss the further benefits of a limited liability partnership.

I will move on to draw some comparisons between S-Corps, C-Corps, and Limited Liability Companies. It is necessary to know what your options are and what advantages an S-Corp has for your particular business. Actual figures hold a lot of importance, and thus I have put together tables with hypothetical figures that are better than written explanations. The breakdown is in terms of different remuneration attracting different percentage tax rates and the tax savings that can be generated.

To take the remuneration considerations further, I will break down what a reasonable salary amounts to and the different ways in which compensation may be paid. I will explain how the IRS scrutinizes tax returns and ways in which they may reallocate seemingly non-wage payments.

There are seven steps that need to be taken in order to successfully set up an S-Corp, and I will list the steps and then explain them in detail. It is very important that you follow the steps in order to prevent mistakes or delays. After the steps, I turn to an explanation of the two main methods of registering an S-Corp: creating an LLC and converting or registering a C-Corp and doing the same. Also included is a list of companies that handle everything involved in the registration of your S-Corp.

Finance for a new business or a cash injection for an existing one is vital, so I have included a section on how to create a list of projected expenses and come to a final figure as to what would be required to set up your S-Corp. While meeting your bank manager in person is somewhat out-dated, it is still possible, so I will go on to explain and recommend more effective ways to obtain business credit. Using a lending marketplace is the best way to go because it allows flexibility, time savings, and expert advice, among other benefits. I also take a look at different types of business credit, such as a small start-up loan, an equipment financing loan, or a business cash advance. I go into enough detail to allow you to understand each type of credit and arm yourself with the knowledge required to use the specific option suited best to your S-Corp.

New business owners can open themselves up to making mistakes. Yes, mistakes are inevitable, but with a sound understanding of the common mistakes that entrepreneurs do make, you can prepare yourself to avoid doing things that may not be helpful to your business. I will take you through a list of mistakes not to make. The list and the expansion under each point are so important, and adhering to them will give you a large advantage over competitors who make the mistakes that you have the knowledge to avoid.

Accounting and tax must be kept up to date, and I do recommend experts in these fields, especially tax. I will stipulate the basics of accounting, such as the general ledger and double entry system, with practical examples. I will take you through the required tax returns—not each and every single line item on the form, but the requirements specific to S-Corps. This is for the purposes of becoming familiar with the form and understanding the different forms of tax payable by S-Corps.

Every business in the US requires a classification code or NAICS code. NAICS stands for the North American Industry Classification System (Pash, 2022). The reason for classification codes is largely for record-keeping and data analysis per sector. I will explain the classifications and how to know which code is used for the different industries.

The next section deals with government work through the GSA (General Services Administration). This can be explained as a mass government contract across the board for suppliers and service providers. It is run via a portal and requires the allocation of and registration for different codes and business identification numbers in order to qualify to receive government contracts. I will explain the different steps and applications required, as well as the benefits of government contracts and subcontracting for other businesses with government contracts. Then I will sum up Doing Business As (DBA), more for information and completeness than direct applicability to S-Corps.

Finally, I will set out practical tips for individuals starting their first business. There are certain things that can be taken for granted or not even considered as one gets wrapped up in parts of the business. It will give you the edge over your competitors, and I would recommend typing them out or writing them down and reading them when you are going through a tough time.

I am confident that this book will leave you in a position with the technical knowledge and practical knowledge to run a successful S-Corp. Please enjoy, and leave a review if you so wish.

CHAPTER 1

S-CORPORATIONS EXPLAINED

Before I can move to S-Corps specifically, it is necessary to paint an overall picture of what a corporation is. Stockholders or shareholders are the individuals that own a corporation, and percentage ownership depends on percentage stock/shareholding. This means that ownership differs depending on the number of shares purchased.

One can see that there is a distinction between a corporation and its owners. Legally, a corporation is considered a person, so for instance, let's say you have two shareholders in a corporation. The total is three people. The shareholders are called natural persons, and the corporation is called a juristic person.

Of course, a corporation is not a living and breathing entity, but it is a separate "person" in terms of the law. Arguably the biggest advantage of being a shareholder in a corporation is that if the corporation goes bankrupt, the person does not. Many decisions as to corporations are based on the legal protection afforded to their shareholders.

A corporation can have a solitary shareholder, meaning that 100% of that corporation is owned by one person. Additionally, a corporation can have as many as 100 shareholders, which means that 100 people each have a percentage share in the corporation. Don't forget that each one of those shareholders has independent rights, as does the corporation.

There are crossovers between corporations, and there are six generally recognized types of corporations, but for these purposes, you need to be aware of three of them. I will cover Limited Liability Companies (LLCs), C-Corporations (C-Corps), and Non-Profit Corporations briefly before moving on to S-Corps in great detail. It is important to understand the basics of LLCs, and C-Corps.

Limited Liability Companies (LLCs)

An LLC can have multiple members or be owned singularly (single-member LLC). LLCs do not require a board of directors and are very flexible in terms of operating requirements and tax filings, meaning that there is a lot less paperwork. Other than that, the attraction is the actual limitation of personal liability, meaning that any personal assets owned in the private name of the LLC owner or owners are safe from repossession in any litigation situation. A slight complication comes in if the LLC has multiple owners, and one of those owners passes away or resigns from the business. That LLC can be dissolved and then re-formed, probably under a different name, if that is the intention of the remaining owner or owners.

C-Corporation Information

A C-Corporation as an entity is completely separate from its owner or owners (Gonzalez, E). A board of directors is required, and the C-Corp is run by the board of directors and the shareholders. C-Corps are subject to double taxation and cannot pass through shareholder profits. This means that the C-Corp is taxed on profits as a corporation, and its shareholders are taxed on the remaining profits as distributed amongst said shareholders. Larger businesses are best served as C-Corps, as it is the appropriate business structure when targeting growth. If you have the intention of working towards offering stock and becoming a public corporation, a C-Corp is the right vehicle for your business. C-Corps also offer the protection of limiting liability, thus ensuring that personal assets are completely separate from assets owned by the C-Corp.

Non-profit Businesses

These types of businesses are not relevant to corporations discussed in this book, but as the name suggests, non-profits just look to cover costs and are most often public-service-orientated, like museums, schools, or hospitals. Charities also fall under this business type, and their taxation rules are largely reduced. Do NOT set up a non-profit business that is actually for profit in order to dodge tax. It is illegal and will have an effect on your future ability to hold corporate positions.

S-Corporations

Before an S-Corp is born, your business must be set up as a corporation by filing what is called "Articles of Incorporation." The aforesaid is a set of legal documentation informing the Secretary of State of the details relevant to your business, such as name, address, and type. Once the corporation is registered, shareholders must sign and submit Form 2553 to make the corporation an S-Corp. From this juncture onwards, taxes are handled individually by each shareholder.

The IRS imposes the following requirements to be met in order to attain S-Corporation status:

- be domiciled in the USA
- have 100 shareholders or less
- have only allowable shareholders
- have only one class of stock
- not be ineligible on any grounds

Be Domiciled in the USA

The simple explanation is that if you don't live in the United States, you cannot be a shareholder. There are a few arbitrary exceptions, such as spending time out of the country working or having a second fixed address in another country. This isn't something to worry about, an expert can provide advice if you do find yourself in a situation similar to the one above.

Have 100 Shareholders or Less

This is self-explanatory but do remember that C-Corps can have over 100 shareholders, so no further information is needed.

Have Only Allowable Shareholders

Certain people and entities are precluded from being shareholders in S-Corps, namely, non-residents, foreign trusts, individual retirement accounts, multiple member LLCs, limited liability partnerships, and C-corps.

Have Only one Class of Stock

Because S-Corps can only have one class of stock, they can only have one class of investors, which can be limiting, as dividends and distribution rights cannot vary outside the equivalence of shareholding. Depending on size, having a 100-shareholder limit may be a disadvantage, and one has to remember that foreign ownership, as well as shareholding by other business vehicles such as trusts, is prohibited.

Not Be Ineligible on any Grounds

This applies to individuals who are still minors, people with criminal records, or any other ineligibility that may arise outside of these categories, such as being under investigation for fraud or having previously declared bankrupt.

Advantages of S-Corps

Protected Assets

All shareholders are exempt from personal liability for any business liabilities or business debt. That means that as a shareholder, your house, car, or any other assets cannot be repossessed in pursuance of money owed by the S-Corp. This exemption can be waived if a shareholder signs as surety on a loan for the business, which is very inadvisable. Asset protection is linked to the S-Corp being its own person, separate from its shareholders, which is not the case for sole proprietorships and general partnerships. Bearing in mind that your personal liability is protected, it would not be a good idea to register personal assets in your S-Corp. For instance, if you register a motor vehicle in the name of the S-Corp, you open yourself up to having that motor vehicle repossessed to cover your business debt if a judgment is obtained against the S-Corp or if bankruptcy is declared.

Pass-through Taxation

Federal taxes do not apply to S-Corps, meaning that any taxation is passed through to the shareholders, who file returns with the IRS in their personal capacity. This is especially useful as losses can offset other personal income, which means less tax. Due to shareholders receiving salaries, the tax is referred to as payroll tax.

Tax-Favorable Characterization of Income

This is basically assigning income to a category. For instance, income may be drawn as a salary by shareholders, or alternatively, dividends can be distributed to the extent that they are tax-free. Running taxation this way allows the reduction of self-employment tax while still generating business expenses and wages paid as deductions for the S-Corp. (CT Corporation Staff, 2022).

Straightforward Transfer of Ownership

Transfer of ownership or shareholding is simple, does not involve property-based adjustments, and does not attract adverse tax consequences. There is no transfer tax or capital gains tax, nor are there any tax penalties (CT Corporation Staff, 2022). This is something that can easily be done by owners or shareholders without professional assistance.

Cash Method of Accounting

Unless an S-Corp has inventory, cash accounting may be used. It is more simple than accrual accounting. The former is a method where receipts are recorded when they are actually received, and expenses are recorded when they are paid. Accrual accounting recognizes an invoice as soon as it is produced, whether it is your company invoicing for services or your company being invoiced. There may come a point where accrual accounting, although more complicated, will be a time saver.

You do get hybrid accounting, which is a mixture of cash and accrual-based accounting, but that will be covered in greater detail later in this book.

Greater Credibility

A sole proprietorship or partnership may give the impression of a small owner-operated business, but an S-Corp evidence professionalism and commitment to the business. Identifying credibility with potential customers, suppliers, and even potential employees is a good way to grow a business effectively. Having said that, it is not a good idea to puff your business up, and you probably shouldn't fake it until you make it, as the saying goes. Honesty and integrity must be maintained.

Disadvantages of S-Corps

Formation and Ongoing Expenses

As mentioned above, you are required to file Articles of Incorporation, which means obtaining a registering agent and paying the associated fee for that person's services. Some states actually impose franchise tax fees and other ongoing fees, such as annual reporting fees. The fees are not outrageous but bear in mind that these fees are not payable by sole proprietors or general partnerships.

Tax Qualification Obligations

Mistakes in terms of filing requirements can cause accidental termination of S-Corp status. This will mean that your S-Corp is taxed as a tax-paying entity under Subchapter C, as above. It doesn't happen often, and it can be corrected, but it is something to be aware of.

The Calendar Year

An S-Corp's tax year must be a calendar year; this is not a major disadvantage, but it can be an admin headache. Appointing a tax expert is a good idea. Such a person does not need to be a full-time employee; however, if your business gets to the point where your taxes become complicated, it may be a good idea to hire someone full-time.

Stock Ownership Restrictions

Because S-Corps can only have one class of stock, it can only have one class of investors, which can be limiting, as dividends and distribution rights cannot vary outside the equivalence to shareholding. Depending on size, having a 100-shareholder limit may be a disadvantage, and one has to remember that foreign ownership, as well as shareholding by other business vehicles such as trusts, is prohibited.

Closer IRS Scrutiny

The IRS pays closer attention to S-Corps, largely because of wages being recharacterized as dividends. The reason for this is that if there is a recharacterization, the S-Corp will be subject to a compensatory deduction. Recharacterization may also work the other way, where dividends are considered wages. This situation makes the S-Corp liable for the employment tax liability.

Less Flexibility in Allocating Income and Loss

Income and/or losses cannot be allocated to shareholders specifically. That is because of one class of stock restrictions (Pierce, M). Stock ownership results in income and loss areas as per percentage shareholding, which is different from partnerships and LLCs, where allocation can be done via the partnership or operating agreement.

Taxable Fringe Benefits in S-Corps

S-Corp shareholders that hold a share portfolio over 2%, are taxed on fringe benefits. Considering that 2% is a very small percentage amount, it is relative to the total number of shareholders.

S-Corp or LLC

S-Corps and LLCs are most closely related to the six generally accepted entities, and the choice between the two may be a difficult one. They both have advantages and disadvantages, and for the purposes of thoroughness, it is important to identify those as well as any overlaps that might sway you from one to the other.

Firstly, the limitation of liability; both types of entities enjoy limited liability, meaning that only assets registered in the name of the entity can be used in bankruptcy to pay any debts or part thereof. It is advisable to limit company assets, and if you are involved in the type of work that doesn't require many assets, then all the better. No person or company wants to go bankrupt; however, shareholders or members of either entity have the peace of mind that if anything does go wrong financially, personal assets are safe from creditors.

Both S-Corps and LLCs have their tax advantages, and taxation on personal income is one of those mutual advantages. LLCs are better suited for sole proprietorships and partnerships, while S-Corps are better suited for businesses with multiple shareholders. That is not to say that a sole proprietor cannot register an S-Corp.

A pro that S-Corps enjoy over LLCs is oversight, which lends itself to greater liability. Because LLCs are a business type, an LLC can also be an S-Corp, the reason being that an S-Corp is a tax classification and not actually a type of business.

Pros and Cons of an S-Corp

Pros

S-Corps do not pay federal taxes, which is a big money-saving opportunity. The professionalism of an S-Corp can go far to establish a good reputation and grow faster than perhaps a sole proprietorship, for example. Employees can receive dividends, which provides for the ability to incentivize and should motivate quality employees, which can only enhance a business.

Cons

There are four states that tax S-Corps as actual corporations: Michigan, California, New Jersey, and New York. So, this would only be a con if you were a resident of such a state. Columbia, New Hampshire, and Tennessee do not recognize S-Corps at all, so like the four states already mentioned, it is only a con if you live in one of the three that do not recognize S-Corps. S-Corps also have a lot of regulations and guidelines to be followed, and as a result of the oversight, the owners and shareholders have less control.

Chapter Summary

Stockholders, otherwise referred to as shareholders are the owners of an S-Corp. Percentage ownership is directly proportional to percentage shareholding. If there are 100 shares and you own 20 shares, that means that you are regarded as a 20% owner. Any confusion or potential disagreements are prevented by this largely practical regulation.

An S-Corp is its own separate person, which means that owners are separate from their S-Corp. Such members cannot exceed 100, and in an S-Corp with, say, 60 shareholders, each shareholder is independent in the same way that a single shareholder is independent. Shareholders enjoy limited liability, meaning that personal assets are exempt from anything having to do with the business. Bankruptcy is the best example, and if it does happen, then shareholders have peace of mind knowing that their assets are safe.

Articles of Incorporation are the set of documentation that must be filed with the Secretary of State, informing the department of the details of your S-Corp. If you are not domiciled in America, you are precluded from being a shareholder. Only one class of stock is permitted, shareholding cannot exceed 100, and potential shareholders must be allowable as shareholders.

The major advantages of an S-Corp are personal asset protection, as well as pass-through taxation. Because federal taxes are inapplicable, losses can offset alternative personal income, which means less tax. If one needs to appoint a new shareholder or if a shareholder wants to sell his or her shares to another person, then the ownership transfer is very simple.

S-Corps are permitted to use cash accounting. That is the recording of transactions as they happen. This is a straightforward method, as opposed to accrual-based accounting, which treats income and expenditure as immediate when an invoice is raised. That means that your books will reflect money that is not yet in your account, so it can become confusing.

Greater credibility is associated with S-Corps due to the business commitment shown and the oversight required.

Expenses are a reality, and when filing Articles of Incorporation, there are fees, which may include agent fees or annual reporting fees. Tax qualification obligations must be understood carefully, and even though they are not complicated, a lack of knowledge could cause errors. The ramifications are the accidental termination of the S-Corp, which thus becomes a tax-paying entity instead of passing through tax to members.

S-Corps have to run the tax year as a calendar year, and it is advisable to get an expert to set that part up. Stock ownership is restricted due to the shareholding being directly proportional to the dividends and distribution rights. Foreign ownership is prohibited, and entities such as trusts cannot be shareholders.

S-Corps are closely scrutinized by the IRS, and there is less flexibility in the allocation of income and loss, compared to a sole proprietorship, as a comparison. Fringe benefits are taxed, and one only has to hold over 2% of shares to be subject to tax on fringe benefits.

S-Corps don't enjoy major advantages over LLCs, but the latter is more suited to sole proprietors and small partnerships. Unfortunately, there are four states in which S-Corps are taxed as corporations and a further three states that don't recognize S-Corps at all.

At this point, you should have a good overview of S-Corps and the information related to them, so I will now turn to their suitability for different types of businesses.

CHAPTER 2

HOW TO KNOW IF AN S-CORPORATION RIGHT FOR YOUR BUSINESS

Businesses are all different; some people sell their time, such as lawyers, accountants, or therapists. Others sell their skills; plumbers or electricians come to mind. In addition, people sell things or provide services, and each of these profit-generating vocations requires the correct business vehicle to best serve the needs of the specific business.

The other big consideration is money; depending on turnover, salaries, expenses, and assets, an S-Corp may or may not be best for your business. Before I turn to look more practically at the money side, it is necessary to briefly touch on the two simplest business types.

The Sole Proprietorship

The name indicates that this type of business vehicle involves only one person, which is correct, but that is not to say that you cannot have other people in the business, i.e., employees. As a sole proprietor, you can have employees, but in terms of tax, the IRS sees you and your sole proprietorship as one and the same. This means that there are no forms to be filled out or registrations to be made; it is just a case of getting on with it. The business owner must file profits or losses with his or her federal tax returns.

The self-employment tax payable includes Social Security and Medicare taxes. There are dangers to a sole proprietorship, but the reason that so many of them exist is because of the zero set-up costs. If you don't have financial resources when starting a brand new business, then setting up an entity with limited liability will be impossible. This means greater risk, but the flip side is that you have complete control, formation is quick, and preparing your tax filings is easy.

The major disadvantage of a sole proprietorship is that if your business goes bankrupt then so do you. Any assets that you own, whether used specifically in the auspices of the business, or otherwise, are at risk. In a bankruptcy scenario, your creditors can repossess anything. If you have a cleaning business and you have bought several sets of industrial cleaning equipment, ownership is seen as no different from ownership of a house or car, or furniture that is not used in the operation of your business. I would argue that the non-existence of liability limitation is a disadvantage too big to ignore. However, certain situations may mean that a sole proprietorship is the only option.

Let's look at some actual figures that should help with your decision. Please note that the figures are not drawn from an actual partnership or S-Corp, they are hypothetical and intended as nothing but an example. The percentages are more important than the turnover, expenses, profits, etc.

Partnership

A partnership is defined as "a formal arrangement by two or more parties to manage and operate a business and share its profits." (Kopp, C). Sharing in profits means that partners also share the liabilities. You do however get silent partners whose liability is limited due to their only contribution being financial. One could say that a partnership with no limited liability is like a sole proprietorship, but it is not only one person that takes on the liability.

You tend to find groups of professionals going into partnership and registering their business as a Limited Liability Partnership (LLP). Doctors or lawyers, for instance, would fit into this category, and one of the larger reasons for operating as an LLP is the possibility of malpractice lawsuits. Let's take a partnership made up of five doctors that share a medical clinic; if one of those doctors botches a procedure and is sued by the patient, and the partnership is not registered with limited liability, all five doctors will share the liability, should the lawsuit be successful.

Tax wise, an LLP is subject to pass-through tax, just like an S-Corp, meaning that partners are taxed in their personal capacity.

I certainly would not recommend a sole proprietorship or partnership above LLCs, C-Corps, and S-Corps, but on the taxation note, I would like to move to salaries, and how they are dealt with in S-Corps.

Reasonable Salaries

As an owner or group of owners, you want your salaries to be as low as possible, without being unreasonable. You can't pay salaries that are unlivable and put personal expenses through your business. Court cases have shown that the salaries must reflect the value of work done by the shareholder/s. Actual personal expenses must be taken into account, but perhaps you are in a situation where your spouse makes enough money to cover your total household expenses. Unfortunately, this doesn't mean that you can draw a minimal salary unless, of course, your value to the S-Corp is equivalent to a low salary. You need to look at the context because every situation is different, but you don't want to get the IRS to start asking questions.

How to Determine What a Reasonable Salary Is

An S-Corp can disguise remuneration as income distribution payments, but that isn't a wise idea, even though it is not strictly illegal. Your salary determination should be factual.

Realistic Compensation

The IRS will scrutinize shareholder-employee compensation. Bear in mind that non-salary distributions by an S-Corp are not taxable as part of payroll taxes. If the IRS does discover distribution payments, they have the power to reclassify the payments as wage payments, which means that they are subject to employment taxes. The reason I say that it is not illegal is that the form of wage payment is actually irrelevant. The declaration and correct classification on your returns is the relevant part. It is still disingenuous to purposefully mislabel wage payments. Once the IRS has done one reallocation, your S-Corp will be flagged, and if the information becomes public, it could cause reputational damage. It should not become public, but often confidentiality is broken.

Officers and Shareholders

There has been litigation challenging the IRS ruling that S-Corp payments to shareholders should be classified in terms of status as officer and shareholder, as opposed to the current classification as an employee. This is unlikely to change, but it is something to keep updated on. After all, you need to know the laws governing your S-Corp and the possibility of those laws being amended.

Family-provided Services

The IRS "punishes" family members for "working for free," or for doing work for the S-Corp and not being adequately compensated. The reason behind a family member assisting and not getting paid may be that the family has other assets that provide remuneration to that family member, such as a real estate portfolio. The IRS will have to determine what a reasonable payment for the services rendered would amount to and allocate tax accordingly. To be clear, a family member is defined by the IRS regulations as "the shareholder's spouse, ancestors, lineal descendants, and any trust of the primary benefit of any of these individuals" (Regs. Sec. 1.1366-3).

What Is Reasonable?

The IRS doesn't specifically define the term "reasonable," but it relies on the gross compensation received by shareholders and non-shareholders as employees for services. The other considerations are capital and equipment. Gross compensation receipts as a result of services rendered by non-shareholder employees, as well as capital and equipment are classified as non-wage distributions to the S-Corp shareholders, meaning that they are not subject to employment taxes. However, if gross compensation receipts are generated by shareholders for direct personal services, they are considered wages and become taxable as employment taxes. If a shareholder-employee offers internal administrative services, such services will not directly produce determinable receipts. For example, if the shareholder employee trains staff in income-generating activities, which the staff then implement, and which in turn create day-to-day receipts, that shareholder is subject to tax on the receipts generated. The IRS uses certain factors more than others when making a determination of what is reasonable; here are the main factors:

1. when bonuses are paid, to whom, and in what manner
2. specific compensation contracts/agreements
3. how much experience employees have (how specialized their role/s are)
4. what the industry-standard compensation is for the job or service provided
5. the S-Corps history of dividend payments
6. salary payments compared to amounts of profit distributed
7. time dedicated to services to the S-Corp
8. duties and responsibilities

Some Hypothetical Numbers

Below is a table with four different examples. The figures are hypothetical, and there is a comparison between a partnership and S-Corps. The percentage savings at the end are what you should focus on because a percentage doesn't change, but actual money/figures do. To explain the table, there is a comparison between a partnership and three salary categories. The fixed amounts for example are revenue, expenses, and profit prior to salaries. The comparison comes in from that point downwards, and the explanation percentagewise follows the table.

	Partner	High Salary	Medium Salary	Low Salary
Revenue per annum	400,000	400,000	400,000	400,000
Expenses per annum	50,000	50,000	50,000	50,000
Profit before salary per annum	350,000	350,000	350,000	350,000
Owner salary per annum	0	250,000	150,000	75,000
Company payroll taxes per annum	0	12,314.80	10,414.80	5,737.50
Profit per annum	350,000	87,685.20	189,585.20	269,262.50
Company payroll taxes brought down	0	12,314.80	10,414.80	5,737.50
Employer payroll taxes brought down	0	12,314.80	10,414.80	5,737.50

Self-employment tax per annum	27,129	0	0	0
Total tax per annum	27,129	24,629.20	20,829.50	11,475
Tax savings per annum	0	2,499.60	6,299.40	15,654

The high salary section leaves only $87,685.20 that does not attract payroll tax, meaning that when compared with a partnership, the tax-saving is 2.9%. Once salaries are kept below the $132,900 mark, the tax-saving benefits are worthwhile for an S-Corp. As before, the salaries have got to be reflective of the work contributions to the business. Highly qualified people such as doctors earn way more than $132,900, and the IRS would raise a red flag if they came across tax returns reflecting much lower salaries than reasonably possible. However, your company may be a high turnover, small profit business, and thus salaries are lower, meaning that the IRS would not raise a red flag at all.

My advice would be to sit with a tax specialist or accountant to go through projected figures on a table similar to the one above before making a decision. Don't lose sight of the limited liability benefit because a small saving might not be worth a lawsuit.

How to Run Payroll

Your salaries have to be structured, even if you are a one-person S-Corp. Technically you can't just take money out of your S-Corp whenever you want to. If you do, however, the IRS will most probably reallocate arbitrary withdrawals for tax purposes. From the table and explanation above, it should be clear that (depending on salary) profits above your salary are taxed at a lower rate.

Use Payroll Services

You will have to pay a monthly fee to a company that offers payroll services, and those services will make things a lot easier. A few days prior to payday, your payroll service will deduct the relevant amount from your business cheque/current account. When payday arrives, you and all other employees will receive your salaries as a payment into your respective personal accounts.

Qualified Business Income (QBI) Deduction

A new tax ruling came out in 2018, allowing business owners to claim a 20 percent deduction on QBI. Salaries that are paid to yourself as part of your S-Corp remuneration allowances do not count, meaning that your QBI deduction will drop quite significantly compared to using a partnership as your business vehicle. I have used the same revenue, expenses, and profit figures as in the table above for the sake of simplicity and only a high salary example to be prudent.

	Partner	High Salary
Revenue per annum	400,000	400,000
Expenses per annum	50,000	50,000
Profit before salary	350,000	350,000
Owner salary	0	250,000
Company payroll taxes per annum	0	12,314.80
Profit per annum	350,000	87,685.20
Qualified business income deduction per annum	70,000	17,537.04

Again, I would advise that you get a tax expert or accountant involved to give you assistance. Paying charges for the correct advice will save money in the long run.

Retirement Plan Options

With S-Corps, the allowable retirement plan contributions are very restricted, especially if you follow the low salary option. With partnerships and sole proprietorships, contributions are based on total income.

Salaries From Other Sources

If you do have a full-time or even half-day job at which you earn a salary, but you are also a shareholder in an S-Corp, the likelihood of paying more taxes is high. However, it is unlikely that you would give up a permanent job to save on tax in your S-Corp, so it is a double-edged sword. Don't lose sight of the fact that employment contracts often preclude employees from earning outside income, so read your contract before making a commitment to an S-Corp.

Let's say that your salaried income is $275,000, and you are paid $50,000 from your S-Corp. Your self-employment tax will be at 2.9%. The reason is that you earn less than the $132,900 cap on your S-Corp income. But the S-Corp will have to pay the full percentage tax rate of 15.3% on your salary, and when you submit your tax return, you can only recover half of that in excess payroll taxes.

This scenario is probably not the best one to be in, but you have to work with actual figures, not just examples, to assess the viability.

S-Corp Versus C-Corp

Comparing these two entities will make your decision easier. The fundamental difference between the two is tax. S-Corps, as we know, are subject to pass-through tax. However, C-Corps are taxed as corporations. There are other differences, and at the outset, you need to know that C-Corps, in most situations, are used by large, staff-heavy entities that trade internationally and rely on foreign investment. That is not to say smaller businesses can't register as C-Corps, so let's have a look at the differences.

Ownership Options

Earlier in the book, I set out the options available to an S-Corp, but they differ when looking at registering a C-Corp. The former can have 100 shareholders or less, one stock class, and no foreign ownership. The latter may have unlimited shareholders, multiple classes of stock, and foreign ownership.

Limited Liability Protection

Both S-Corps and C-Corps have limited liability, so either way, there is personal peace of mind.

Pass-Through versus Corporate Tax

This is dependent on the size of your entity, but pass-through tax is a big plus in an S-Corp. Also, don't lose sight of the fact that the C-Corp tax rate is 21%, which is very high. However, the actual monetary tax amount will differ depending on the taxable amount.

Dealing With Losses

As we know, S-Corps can declare losses to offset shareholder income, whereas that option is not open to C-Corps. Many businesses run at losses, and in fact, the popular opinion is that a new business is likely to run at a loss for the first three years. Obviously, a loss is non-taxable, and you do get cases where accountants fiddle with the figures to reflect losses. NEVER do this; it really is not worth going to jail for bending tax laws.

Profit Distribution

With S-Corps, distribution is according to shareholding, based on the one class of stock requirement. C-Corps are not restricted in any way and may distribute profits by dividends, as well as by issuing shares. The latter is useful in attracting investors, and the flexibility assists in the credibility of the C-Corp.

S-Corp Suitability

- when you want to draw profits as income
- when you are able to benefit from losses
- to have a low personal income tax rate
- when you want to actively participate in day-to-day running

C-Corp Suitability

- when you have a foreign interest or want to pitch your business to potential overseas investors
- if you want to reinvest profit
- if you want unlimited growth potential (more than 100 shareholders)
- if you want different types of shareholders, such as trusts, other C-Corps, or international equivalents to U.S. corporates
- if you have owners with high personal tax rates
- if you want to attract local investors as well as foreign investors

Chapter Summary

There are different types of businesses, which means that business structures vary across different types of businesses. For example, a doctor or group of doctors is unlikely to structure its business in the same way that a logistics company does.

Money is a big deciding factor, and looking at actual figures is a good way to get valid information in order to make the decision as to whether an S-Corp is best suited to your business.

The lack of limited liability in sole proprietorships leaves the sole proprietor open to liability for all assets used in business activities or private activities. New business owners are sometimes left with no choice but to operate as sole proprietors due to limited funds, but the option to register an LLC or S-Corp at a later stage is always there.

Partnerships are not advisable because liability is not limited. A partnership can be registered as a Limited Liability Partnership (LLP), which is most often used by professionals, such as accountants or lawyers.

Salary amounts are impacted by the tax, depending on thresholds. For instance, a salary below the cap of $132,900 attracts a tax rate of 2.9%. However, the IRS requires that salaries are in proportion to work done or the value of the business. Take the doctor example; a doctor is worth way more than $132,900, and if that doctor was drawing a salary under the cap, the IRS is likely to have questions. The two tables with figures set out in this chapter should be very useful in calculating the best financial structure. Retirement plans are important, and S-Corps restrict contributions, so you have to weigh up the factors, including this one.

It is possible to have a salary from a job and still be a shareholder who draws a salary from an S-Corp. This is dangerous territory and could result in higher overall taxation.

An alternative to an S-Corp is a C-Corp, both of which have advantages and disadvantages, and overlaps. Both have limited liability, but S-Corps have restrictions as to the number of shareholders and are not allowed to have overseas shareholders.

C-Corps are much less restrictive, as they have unlimited shareholding options and are permitted to have foreign investors. This doesn't mean that C-Corps are an automatic best choice; it is a subjective choice depending on your business type. If you want to reinvest profit, issue multiple stock shares, and you want to attract investors, then a C-Corp is the way to go. If you want to draw benefits from losses and also draw profits, in addition to minimizing tax, then an S-Corp is your answer.

Don't forget that the money side of the decision should be explored with a tax expert or accountant, and do remember that a fee for such professional advice will probably save you money when your business is fully operational.

At this point, you should have a more specific understanding of S-Corps and an understanding of their suitability for your business. It is time to continue onto the actual formation of your S-Corp and the steps that you need to take to do so.

CHAPTER 3

STARTING YOUR S-CORP

You have made your decision, and you are ready to get going. This chapter will guide you through the steps required and give advice on what to do within each step to make the process as easy as possible. There is, of course, the option of appointing an expert in the field, and as I have said before and will say again, money spent on such will very likely save money in the long run.

Step 1: Decide on a Unique Name for Your Business

A name should get across what the business actually does. Avoid meaningless titles like CRF Services or BTR Proprietors, or Hanson Brothers. Rather choose a name such as CRF Accounting Services if your business is an accounting firm. BTR Real Estate Proprietors if your business is an estate agency and Hanson Brothers Furniture if your business is a furniture retailer.

Step 2: Check if the Name is not Already Taken by Another Business

You don't want your name to sound similar or be exactly the same as an existing business. Most businesses have an online presence, so use Google to search your proposed names and see if your business name will clash with others. You might want to go for a cheesy pun or something that rhymes or a different take on spelling, in order to grab the attention of potential customers. Something like "Movers and Shakers Furniture Transport" or "No Shorts Electrical."

Step 3: Choose the State in Which You Intend to Form Your S-Corp

You should remember that in chapter 1, I listed the four states in which S-Corps do not have pass-through tax: Michigan, California, New Jersey, and New York. These states tax S-Corps as corporations, and the following states do not recognize S-Corps at all: Columbia, New Hampshire, and Tennessee. Most often, S-Corps will be registered in the state where they are domiciled. Domicile is the address from which your C-Corp trades.

If your S-Corp is completely online operated then Delaware is the best state in which to form the S-Corp. The process is the easiest out of all the states, the tax rates and tax benefits are very favorable, and the state offices are helpful and efficient.

Step 4: File and Submit the S-Corp's Articles of Association/Incorporation

Below is an example of what articles of incorporation will look like. You can draft and complete the document yourself, but using a professional will eliminate possible errors.

ARTICLES OF INCORPORATION OF:

ABC FURNITURE REMOVALS

Under the Business Corporation Laws of the state of Delaware.

The name of the corporation is ABC Furniture Removals.

The principal place of incorporation is _____

The name and address of the registered agent is _____

The purpose for which the incorporation is organized is

_____

The corporation is authorized to issue X amount of shares:

Without a par value of ____ or without a par value (2022) .

Names and addresses of all directors are as follows (legaltemplates, n.d.):

_____

_____

Names and addresses of all financial officers are as follows (legaltemplates, n.d.):

_____

_____

The name and address of the incorporator is:

_____

The period of duration of the corporation is (legaltemplates, n.d.):

Perpetual or X number of years or ends on X date.

Executed, signed, and witnessed on the X date of X month, X year.

_____

Signature of shareholder/s

_____

Witness signature

Step 5: Determine the Board of Directors

The board of directors can comprise all of the shareholders or some of the shareholders, and the limit is 100 individuals. It is very unlikely that every single one of the 100 shareholders will be a member of the board of directors in an instance where there is such a vast number of shareholders, but it is possible.

Step 6: Keep Minutes of all Shareholder Meetings and Board Meetings

When any decision affecting the running of the S-Corp is made, it needs to be recorded by the shareholders, and/or board of directors in an officially chaired meeting. The meeting need not be formal or lengthy as long as the important and prevalent parts of the meeting are noted and recorded.

Step 7: Get an Employer Identification Number (EIN) and File a Form 2553 to Elect S-Corp Tax Status

An EIN is your Employer Identification Number, which you will obtain on application from the IRS. When you have been allocated your EIN, you will need to complete form 2553. The form can be downloaded from the IRS website or obtained from your local IRS office. It is the form on which you apply for shareholders to be subject to individual tax.

There is some repetition from the articles of association across form 2553, but for the sake of completeness, this is the information required on form 2553:

- The name of your business
- The physical address of your business
- Your EIN
- The state in which you wish your S-Corp to be registered in
- The date of incorporation
- The effective date of the S-Corp election
- A complete list of all shareholder information
- A comprehensive set of information on your fiscal tax year
- All shareholders signatures

You will also require a witness to the signatures. An outside party can be a witness, but nobody involved in the set-up of the S-Corp can act as a witness. An employee or non-shareholder is permitted to be a witness, and do remember that the witness is a witness to the signature and nothing else.

A look at the two Main Ways to Set up an S-Corp

LLC

Form an LLC first, then select your S-Corp tax status from the IRS, after which, request your Employer Identification Number (EIN). The steps to set up an LLC are very similar to the steps to set up an S-Corp, so I am not going to go into great detail. Here they are, in shortened form, followed by the three types of conversions:

- Choose the name
- Check that the name is available
- Choose the state
- Appoint a registered agent
- Fill in and file the articles of organization (almost the same as articles of association)
- Prepare and file the form
- Draw up an operating agreement

My advice is if you intend using this method, you should try to get both forms and fill them in at the same time, with professional assistance.

Statutory Conversion

Depending on your state, you can do a "quick-status" conversion, in which you will fill in the forms, and submit them to the secretary of state. The time periods are short, and as the name suggests, the status change does not take long.

Statutory Merger Information

This option gives you the chance to merge your existing LLC into a new corporation. First, you will create the new corporation and then have a vote involving LLC members for approval to change the members to shareholders. If this is a decision, it will be made as a group, so the election could very well be simple, hands up for yes, count the votes, hands up for no and count the votes. The final step is to file a certificate of merger, available from the office of the secretary of state or the IRS website.

Non-statutory Conversion

You will require lawyers and accountants if you use this method, which can make it expensive. It is also a complicated process, as you are required to create the corporation and then transfer any assets and liabilities that your existing LLC has in its name, and then liquidate the LLC, and dissolve it.

C-Corp

C-Corps differ from LLCs and S-Corps, more than S-Corps differ from LLCs, but I will still go into the relevant details. Naming your business and checking that the name is available remains the same. Next, you need to arrange your leadership by appointing shareholders and directors. Then, file the articles of association and issue stock certificates. Finally, apply for the requisite business licenses and/or permits. When all the paperwork is done, you can then convert to an S-Corp.

Using a Company to Create Your S-Corp

I have mentioned previously that hiring a tax expert or an accountant would be a good idea, but using a single company to do everything as a one-stop shop is probably the easiest way to do it. As with any commercial service, costs vary greatly, but cheap and expensive are relative to your budget or the budget of your S-Corp. I have compiled a list of ten companies through experience and research. My choices are based on the most user-friendly website, the quality of the service, and whether or not the fees are reasonable. The list is in no particular order, and all of the companies are easily findable with a simple Google search.

On the question of fees, you will notice that several of the above companies state just their fee on their website but do not include fees payable to the state registering authority. Other companies state the full price, which includes their fee and the registration fees with the state department. Be aware of these factors when you are exploring and deciding which service to go with.

Financing Your S-Corp

Nobody likes to create debt, and doing so can be a source of tremendous stress and worry. However, sometimes it can be inevitable, and other than the set-up costs of an S-Corp in terms of registration, you may need to put deposits down for office rental, furniture, equipment, and other unavoidable costs. Banks and financiers often have credit plans specifically for new businesses. To work out how much money you require upfront, you should make lists of exactly what you need and the costs thereof, get to a final figure, and then put on a 20% contingency for any unforeseen costs. It is a good idea to put together a complete business plan, with the numbers on a spreadsheet, so when you approach an institution for finance, they can see that you have your ducks in a row and that you intend to succeed. Banks don't (shouldn't) dish out loans to anyone, so the impression that you make on behalf of your S-Corp is very important.

Every year Forbes puts out a list of business financiers with ratings of four and five out of five stars. It is definitely worth having a look at these lists and deciding on which institution will work best for you. There is another option, which I would argue is the best one, and that is the lending marketplace, which does not restrict you to one institution. If you have a range of options that are easily attainable, it can only benefit your power of choice.

Business Lending Marketplace

What follows are five essentials that any businessperson interested in financing a new business or giving an existing business a cash injection needs to know. Don't just brush over these; they are vital in planning financially.

You Are not Restricted to one Option

Let's say hypothetically that you want to buy a car. You are not going to walk into the first dealership, pick one out and buy it. Most people will look around, go to more than one dealership and find the best deal. The same should apply to finding a business loan.

A lending marketplace allows you to compare loan amounts, repayment periods, interest rates, and the amount of time it takes to have a loan approved. It is a bit like using a site that allows you to book flights across multiple airlines based on all the information on that one site. Don't lose sight of the fact that cheaper may not always be beneficial, do your homework properly.

Flexibility

Your S-Corp may be in a position where it will require a short-term loan to make a bulk stock payment in order to take advantage of a rebate from a supplier, or you may need to take a long-term loan to set up your infrastructure. Being able to choose from a variety of options gives you the tools to find the best lending strategy for what you specifically require.

Time-Saving

You do not have to fill out an application for every single credit provider. A lending marketplace allows access to offers from several lenders. All you have to do is complete the necessary forms online and hit the submit button.

Expert Guidance

The teams on lending marketplace websites are trained and qualified to answer any questions that you may have. You don't have to restrict yourself to just one lending marketplace before you make decisions that best suit your S-Corp.

Speed and Size

Sometimes you need a small loan fast. Other times you may be looking for a larger loan, and you have more time to explore options. With a small loan, the interest rate may not be that important, but rather fast access to money may be the main deciding factor. When looking for a larger loan, you will probably have more time to explore different options, especially when it comes to the interest rates.

Types of Loans

As touched on previously, different businesses require different types of loans. Here are some options to be aware of.

Business Line Credit Option

This is a type of loan that you only use when you actually need to. It is available all the time, set to a limit, depending on what you qualify for. It can lay dormant for six months if you don't require its use, but you can draw on it quickly if you require cash for whatever business purpose. You only pay interest on what you use. Repayment terms and plans differ from credit provider to credit provider, which is another reason to use lending marketplaces to make a decision.

Small Business Loans

A small business loan is finite in that it has a specific term, a specific interest rate, or an interest rate linked to the prime lending rate, and is for a specific amount of time. This is the original type of business loan that has existed since banks began lending money. Your decision in this instance will be based not necessarily on how many shareholders you have, but on the size of the business relative to setup costs.

Business Cash Advance

Any loan has a form of risk attached to it, but this one carry substantial risk. A business cash advance requires future collateral that is provided via profit projections. Once you are granted your advance, the pressure is on, but at the end of the day, you want to make money, so maybe the pressure is a good thing.

Equipment Financing

Whether you need a tractor, an industrial dishwasher, or a set of smart tables and chairs for your boardroom, you can apply to finance that equipment. Now, remember that if you do not make your repayments, the equipment may be subject to repossession.

I hope at this stage you are thinking back to the limiting of liability, and you would be right to do so. Sometimes there is no choice but to put assets purchased into the S-Corps name, but when you take this option, be very careful to make sure that you will meet the repayments.

Business Start-up Loan

This type of loan will most likely not require collateral, although that is not the case in every situation. It is what it is called and is used to start up a new business from the ground up.

Short-Term Loan

This kind of credit is best suited to situations when your S-Corp needs money and needs it fast. A short-term loan is processed in a few minutes and often pays out within 24 hours. Generally, full payment is required within a specified period. So let's say a supplier has offered you an upfront payment discount, and you have a buyer for the product but are short on cash. Then you take the loan out, buy the stock, sell it and repay the loan with the proceeds of the sale. A short-term loan can be used to your advantage in a situation like the above.

Commercial Mortgage

If you want to buy the premises from which you will be operating your business, a mortgage is the way to go. Very few new businesses or even existing businesses can afford to buy immovable property in cash. One specific advantage is that as time goes by and you start creating equity in the S-Corp's property, you can borrow further to do renovations or additions.

Accounts Receivable Financing

I would not advise any business to take this option. Basically, the financier will pay your S-Corp a percentage of your customer invoices up front, usually somewhere around 80%, but when your customer/s pay the invoice, the financier takes a share. Usually, the share is 3–5%. It seems good on principle, but whether or not your customers pay on time, late, or not at all, the financier will come running for their percentage very quickly. I'm not saying that this option doesn't work, but I see the risk as quite high. It does, of course, depend on the individual situation of the S-Corp, so in some instances, it may be riskier than others, but just be cautious on this one.

Small Business Administration Loan (SBA)

This is a business loan partially backed by the government. The SBA does not actually provide the cash but rather establishes guidelines for loans and provides guarantees for certain portions of those loans.

Operating Agreement

It is wise to have an operating agreement, to manage expectations and make sure that all shareholders are absolutely clear on the important aspects of the business. Below is a sample of an operating agreement (Upcounsel, 2020). It is not too complicated to draw one up, and you can get templates on various free document sites.

Operating Agreement Between

XYZ S-Corp

And

Shareholder One

And

Shareholder Two

This operating agreement is entered into between Shareholder One and Shareholder Two, as members, and XYZ S-Corp, as the company, on the following terms:

The name of the business is XYZ S-Corp, and is situated at 123 First Avenue.

The purpose of the business is to operate lawfully as a Limited Liability S-Corp, as a furniture manufacturer and fitment business.

This agreement will take effect on X date and run indefinitely, until such time as the S-Corp is dissolved, for whatever reason whatsoever.

All certificates or documents requiring publication will be published after this agreement has been signed.

The members have agreed to each put forward $10,000 as start-up capital, the total being $20,000, as the total contribution from the two shareholders.

The annual net income or net loss shall be allocated to the members each fiscal year.

Members may sell, assign or transfer shareholding in the company, but not before written consent from the other shareholders.

If the shareholders resolve to dissolve the business, the members will take full account for the assets and liabilities of the company and will liquidate the assets within a reasonable time period and at an amount/s consistent with reasonable market value.

The business shall be member-managed.

Amendments will only be valid when placed in writing. This document comprises the entire operating agreement.

_____   _____

Signature of shareholder/s   *Signature of shareholder/s*

_____

Witness signature

Chapter Summary

When you have decided that you want to start an S-Corp, there are seven steps that you need to follow, as set out above. Choose a name that is not already taken, and that is not similar to an existing business and then pick the state in which you want to register your S-Corp. Draft your C-Corps Articles of Association, as per the example set out under step four. Establish your board of directors and from the first meeting, record everything discussed in every meeting. Apply for your employer identification number and when received, fill in form 2553, to elect your tax status.

Be aware of the information required on the said form, as per the bullet points under step seven, and the two main ways of setting an S-Corp, i.e., LLC conversion or C-Corp then to S-Corp. Consider an expert to take care of all the steps for you, and remember that paying an expert will probably save you money in the longer term, and ensure that the process runs smoothly. Pay attention to the ten listed companies that I recommended and jump on Google for more information on their services.

Financing is something to think about, and it is vital to arrive at a figure that covers absolutely everything, then add a contingency for miscellaneous expenses, and come to a grand total. From that point, you can explore which financing option is best for your S-Corp. Business lending marketplaces give you information on several loans and credit options, which you can access by doing just one application.

There is a diverse range of financing options, from the government-backed SBA loan system to commercial mortgages, if your S-Corp intends to buy offices or premises. When you are considering what will serve your S-Corp best, don't forget the importance of limited liability. I believe that this chapter will have given you peace of mind that you know how to get your S-Corp to the point of readiness to trade and that you have an understanding of choosing the correct set-up and financing route suited best to your S-Corp.

The final part of the chapter is an example of an operating agreement. It is a very simple one but gives you an accurate idea of what one looks like.

CHAPTER 4

WHAT NOT TO DO

I f you are starting a business for the very first time, the setup can be seen as a teaser to a movie, and the real start is your first day of trading. Things can go wrong, so let's take a dive into some advice about what not to do.

There are several reasons that businesses fail, and a sad fact is that already established businesses could not survive the economic restrictions that the COVID-19 pandemic imposed. In that sense, business closures were, and continue to be unavoidable.

If you have a relatively new business or are starting one soon, whether it is an S-Corp or not, you need to pay attention to taking care of the aspects that are within your control.

More than 18% of new businesses fail in the first two years, and more than 55% do not get past the five-year mark. By reading this book and taking note of what follows, the chances of your business succeeding are doubled, perhaps even tripled.

Mistakes to Avoid When Starting Your Business

Being Afraid to Fail

We hear this often (Schooley, 2022). There is a difference between being nervous and being afraid. Don't let thoughts of failure enter your mind. We also often hear the recommendation of having a plan B or not putting all your eggs in one basket. However, if you only have a plan A, you have the motivation to succeed. There will be setbacks, no business that has ever existed has run smoothly all the time; it is just not possible. Expect that things will go wrong, but do not dwell on that. Do everything you can, and if you face a bump in the road, deal with it when it happens.

Not Making a Business Plan

The cheesy saying, "failing to plan, is planning to fail," is so true. You can't just throw yourself into a project without knowing what you are doing. You will learn as you go, but having a comprehensive plan should allow you to do as much as you can from the get-go.

Being Disorganized

People seem to think that if you are disorganized, then that is that, but if you have a propensity for disorganization, it can be changed. Get a diary; keep physical files as well as electronic ones. Keep a diary, and don't leave tasks, do them immediately. Procrastination also falls into this category. Make sure you display organization and immediacy from day one of trading your S-Corp. It isn't that difficult!

Not Defining Your Target Market

If you don't know who you are selling to then you are going to struggle to sell. You may have a very niche market. Let's say your S-Corp supplies a specialized type of heavy-duty screw used on 34-tonne trucks. That market is very specific, so you need to tailor advertising and marketing campaigns toward logistics companies and fleet owners. If you sell dishwashing liquid, your potential market is huge, but you need to be unique and reasonably priced. It is probably more difficult to sell dishwashing liquid than a specific type of hardware used in the trucking industry. You can include these details in your business plan, or you can develop a separate marketing plan.

Not Filing for the Appropriate Business Type/Classification

What you have read up until now has given you all the knowledge and tools to get your S-Corp going, so at this point, you are aware that this is the correct type of business vehicle for your purposes.

Trying to Do Everything Yourself

Starting a business on your own can be intimidating, and while you should avoid thinking about failure, keep in mind that there are people who can assist you. Not necessarily with the actual running of your business, but with aspects of it. Our networks in this day and age are really big, and one can always find a friend of a friend who is willing to help. Think about it like this; when (not if) you become a successful entrepreneur, it would be wonderful if you could help up-and-comers in your field. That means that there are successful people that are in such a position now. Paying experts to do something in a few days that would take you a week is something to consider. Perhaps your forte is sales, but you're not great at Excel. You could hire someone to work one morning a week, perhaps a retired accounting teacher who is looking for something to occupy themselves.

Getting the Wrong Investors

Without a doubt, there are people out there who will scam you and try and make a quick buck or investors that will put what looks like a great deal on the table, only for you to discover that it isn't that great after business commences. If it sounds too good to be true, it probably is (Schooley, 2022). Your business is like your child. You want to nurture it and guide it as it grows and begins to succeed. Only partner with people or institutions that have the same outlook. In the previous chapter, we looked at financiers, but those were bigger players in finance. I am talking about smaller investors. I'm not saying don't explore offers or opportunities, but on this one, it is very advisable to have a lawyer look over any contract before you put pen to paper.

Avoiding Contracts

A he said/she said situation can easily be prevented if you put everything down in writing. A so-called "gentlemen's agreement" may have business romanticism to it, but this is the time to be cynical. You can't make a supply deal over the phone and then fail to put the terms in writing thereafter. If something goes wrong, you are going to want to produce written proof in order to settle whatever disagreement may arise.

Hiring too Soon

There must be a mix between doing everything yourself and hiring others to do so. A new business doesn't start with a decent cash flow in the first month, so do as much as you can with the time you have. The time to start hiring is when you become too busy to attend to every part of the running of your business. As I said, it is a mix, and some services you will have to pay for, even if you are not busy yet. Take the Excel example above and apply that to this tip as well.

Understanding Capital Requirements

As I said in the previous chapter, when you calculate your set-up costs, you need to build in a contingency. I suggest 20% because there will be unforeseen costs. For instance, you need an industrial printer, and you are under the impression that the ink is part of the cost. You discover that such is not the case, and now your budget is out, but not if you have built-in that contingency. You want to avoid going back to the bank or financier a second time to increase your start-up loan.

Wasting Money

Your product must be the best it can be, but you don't need brand-new hardwood furniture, a TV in the boardroom, and a fancy coffee machine. Those things can come later in your journey.

Focus on what is important, i.e., a good product or service and an effective marketing strategy.

Paying Yourself the Wrong Salary

You should remember the table in chapter 3, setting out a partnership versus an S-Corp, comparing low, medium, and high salaries. Refer back to that, as getting the salary correct, within a range of course, in order to minimize tax, is vital. Even if your business starts increasing its turnover rapidly, don't take too much money out. Rather, pay off your startup loan or other chosen financing.

Undervaluing or Overvaluing Your Product/Service

Among other things, your goal is to make money, but don't be greedy. If you are the most expensive product on the market, your product must be extremely unique and your service must be exceptional. Some companies do indeed use service as their draw card. Also, don't cut your margins to an amount that will see to it that you have to sell way more of your product than is actually possible to make a decent amount of money. Investigate what your competitors are charging, do your homework, and set your pricing at a fair value. If people feel that they are getting fair value for money, that is when your product starts selling itself, and your quality of service is spread by word of mouth.

Launching too Quickly

You need to check and double-check that all aspects of the business are ready before you launch. As an example, you have been talking to a potential customer about signing a supply contract when you launch, and everything seems to be on track. The contract is not yet signed, but it is the last thing that needs to be done before you can start to manufacture your product. Even though the signature has not hit the page you decide to push play on the manufacture, which brings with it certain expenses. Your thinking is that by the time the product is ready, the contract will be signed, and your business will be off to a good start. You do a big launch and set the marketing wheels in motion, only to discover that the potential customer has gone with another supplier. So you sit with an excess of stock, which you have paid for, and nobody to sell it to. The point is that you need to make sure everything is in place before you launch. This is just an example of many possibilities. As I said before, things do go wrong, but as I also said, control the things that you can control. It is understandable that the emotions associated with that first deal may tempt you to press go before you are ready, but hang on until you really are ready.

Expanding too Quickly

If you experience initial success, which I hope you do, that doesn't mean that you need to hire a bunch of staff straight away and move to bigger premises. Expansion should come when you and your fellow shareholders do not have time to attend to everything required in running a successful business. Your balance sheet is also important, in that if you can employ someone to take care of managing manufacture, to allow you to get out into the market and attend to the promoting and selling of your product, in order to make more money, then the time for expansion has come. Don't fall into the trap of securing one contract and having grandiose ideas of immediate economic growth, then hiring a bunch of people that may end up sitting around half the day. Expanding does not only refer to taking on staff but also to taking on tasks that your fledgling business does not have the capabilities of doing just yet. Hypothetically, you distribute chipboard used in the manufacture of cheap cupboards, your first order is small, and you deliver 1 ton of the chipboard. Your customer is impressed and asks you to deliver 10 tons. You know you don't have the capabilities to meet the delivery deadline. DON'T just say "yes" and then figure it out later. Rather be honest and tell the customer that you have to do X, Y, and Z before you can fulfill an order that big. Honesty is appreciated, and I am sure that said customer will perhaps order another ton, but ask you to aim at 10 tons per month, six months from the date. At that point, you can do what needs to be done, in order to fulfill the customers 'requirements. Don't forget to sign a supply contract first! (I will carry on repeating this one, it is very important).

Not Doing Proper Bookkeeping

Absolutely everything needs to be correctly recorded. In your first month, perhaps you have only a few transactions, and it is easy to record them. In month two there are a few more, but you put off doing your spreadsheet until the month after, as you are focusing on sales. By the time you get around to recording the transactions, your bank statement reflects items that you don't remember, and it takes you far too long to search for invoices and to pinpoint what charges are what. Don't let it get away from you! This is why physical files are important. Keep every single slip and invoice and estimate and anything else that involves money coming in and out. You want to be able to do your own books for as long as possible before paying someone to do them. There will be cases where you need a bookkeeper from day one, but even then, you need to keep slips, invoices, etc., to give to your bookkeeper so that he or she stays on top of recording all transactions. There is nothing worse than "tax season" arriving and having to spend hours getting copies of invoices and trawling through months of bank statements to identify unrecorded transactions.

Not Coming up With a Marketing Plan

As we all know, marketing is huge. If nobody knows about your product or service, then nobody is going to buy your product or use your service. Marketing differs depending on what your business does, but below is an adaptable outline of what a marketing plan should look like.

Your Business's Mission

Take a joinery and fitment company as an example: "We aim to provide all-inclusive fitment solutions, from first measure to final installation." You can also use the mission or part of it as a tagline for your business, "ABC joinery, from measure to perfection."

Define your Key Performance Indicators

Key Performance Indicators or KPI's are the metrics used to judge the who, how, and what of marketing. The most obvious example is online marketing, so tracking your social media likes, views and comments can give you an idea of what marketing content is receiving a positive response. In the joinery market, there will be expos and trade shows that you can target as part of your exposure campaign. Word of mouth is even a metric that can be defined. For instance, get customers to fill out a short survey form and gather that information to hone in on what works for your target market.

Identify the Type of Person That Wants Your Product

One way to get this information is via your KPI's, but also via understanding what demographic likes your product. Perhaps you manufacture sportswear, and a major product is trendy lycra yoga pants for women. Your target market would likely be young, sporty women that are health and fashion-conscious.

Record Your Marketing Strategy

This can be in list or point form and may look something like this:

- Summer trade shows
- Advert in XYZ magazine
- Customer feedback forms
- Mailing list
- YouTube content campaign
- Blog

The above isn't specific to any one type of business, just a basis for how to form a strategy.

What not to Focus On

You know what your target market is, so you can identify the demographic that you are not targeting. You don't want to waste your marketing budget on a demographic that has no need or use for your product.

Record Your Budget

It is vital to know how much money you have available and to what elements of marketing it is allocated. Be specific and remember that even if you have a limited budget, there are a whole lot of free marketing opportunities.

Identify Your Competition

You need to know who and/or what you are trying to out-market and out-sell. You can also learn from your competition. If you don't know anything about your competitors, they already have the edge over you.

Hiring the Wrong People

A formal interview is the most commonly used hiring method, but remember, prospective employees, are going to tell you what they think you want to hear. We often misjudge people, thinking that we have found the right person for the job, only to discover that such isn't the case. If you think about it, someone who is unemployed needs to find a job to generate an income. That means that such a person will cast the net wide, and send his/her resume to as many companies as possible. Their objective may be to secure the first job that they can, to get an income, and then carry on applying for the job that they really want.

Do as many checks as you can before making a decision on staff. Very often, employers will choose employees based on an interview without getting hold of that person's references. It is generally accepted that a resume contains the contact details of former employers, so contacting them isn't difficult and should not be overlooked.

Over-Promising and Under-Delivering

Don't put yourself in a situation where you commit to a date and then cannot deliver on or before that date. Simply put, under-promise and over-deliver. Give yourself some breathing room to allow for unforeseeable delays. If you fail to meet a commitment, you will look very bad, and in those cases, word travels fast.

Failing to Understand the Demands of Business

When you go into a new venture, expect to work hard, expect early mornings and long days, expect stress, and never think it will be easy. If you are an employee, you have one job, but as an owner or shareholder, there is a lot to get done. When the clock ticks over to 5 p.m., that doesn't mean that you can go home. You have to do what needs to be done to drive your business toward success. If you are half-hearted about your business, it will never work.

Chapter Summary

Statistics show that a large portion of new businesses fails. The possible mistakes set out in this chapter are to make sure that your business is not among the adverse statistics. Not only you have to have a plan, work hard, and be organized, but you also have to know when the time comes to hire people. When you can't get through all your work day to day, and your business starts to suffer, you require help, and it is out there. Be cautious, though. Avoid the wrong investors and make sure you understand your capital requirements. Don't dive in too quickly, also don't hire too quickly. Make sure you know your target market, and your competitors. Include these things in your marketing plan, keep your books up to date, and be prepared to put in the hard yards. The contents of this chapter are as important, if not more important, than the administrative side of your S-Corp set-up, so please, I urge you to take them to heart.

CHAPTER 5

ACCOUNTING AND TAX FOR YOUR S-CORP

A ccounting/bookkeeping are important, and tax forms are scary, but don't panic. Below is an explanation of both so you have an idea of what it all entails before you have that first meeting or interview with your prospective accounting and tax expert.

Your S-Corp will receive invoices and issue invoices. An invoice is basically a list of things sold or services given, with an amount payable for such things or services. It is important to use a numbering system or reference system so that you can easily locate invoices when required.

An invoice should contain the name of your S-Corp, or trading name, as well as your S-Corp's address and your customer's name and address. Furthermore, an invoice must have your S-Corps banking details and instructions on how to pay. A clear reference number must be printed onto the invoice, and in the payment instructions, you must request that the customer stipulates the reference number when making payment. This makes it a lot easier to allocate payment receipts to specific payments and prevents the need to trawl through pages of bank statements to reconcile invoices. An invoice does not have to be complicated or have unnecessary information. The next paragraph is the rough wording of an invoice, but there are many ways to set out the information on a written document.

Invoice from: XYZ Corp, 123 First Avenue, Nutbush, on X date 2022, to ABC Housing, 456 Second Avenue, Nutbush. For: Plumbing services rendered on Y date 2022, in the amount of $500, due on or before Z date 2022. XYZ Corp's banking details are PayPal xxxxxx. When making payment, please use reference number 135-Ab, to allow us to allocate the payment.

Your S-Corp will also receive invoices that should have the above information; it really is just the layout that will change. After payment, then a receipt is raised as proof that the invoice has been paid.

Receipt of: $500 paid by ABC Housing, 456 Second Avenue, Nutbush, to XYZ Corp, 123 First Avenue, Nutbush, on X date 2022, for plumbing services rendered on Y date 2022, allocated under reference number 135-Ab.

How to Keep Accounting Records

The basic principles of bookkeeping are an accepted set of uniform rules in general, but depending on your entity and your choice of taxation, they will differ slightly. Financial statements will be scrutinized at your shareholder's meeting, if you have more than one shareholder. The information contained therein must be specific and as correct as possible. It is not uncommon that the S-Corps financial statements will need to be adjusted slightly. Smaller things, such as recording the purchase of office fungibles as a petty cash expense when they were actually purchased with the company credit card, and similar transactions, occur frequently. As long as the money in and money out are correct on your balance sheet, the finer details can be corrected with no problem. Here are the basics that you need to do:

Collect and Capture

It sounds self-explanatory, but it is the DOING that is important. The "collect" means to collect any proof of transaction, i.e., sales invoices, copies of checks, and even slips for small day-to-day purchases. Absolutely everything! Avoid cash-in-hand transactions without any proof, but if you do, then record the transaction immediately. My advice is to open files and file copies of everything. If your S-Corp is a grocery store, it is likely that every till will produce a print-out every day as part of the point-of-sale system. If you neglect to record the transactions and/or file them, even if your system generates the same, you will fall behind and create more work for yourself or your accountant/bookkeeper.

Your General Ledger

If I had a dollar for every time, I heard the term "general ledger," I would be a wealthy man. However, the common use of the term indicates that it is an accounting document that garners regular use. General ledgers use the double-entry system of accounting and are often kept quarterly, but I prefer to keep them monthly or even weekly if you are passing a significant amount of transactions. Here is a very simple example that will give you the basics of what a general ledger is. I am only going to include one expense (weekly rent) to keep it just to the fundamentals.

Note that week one and week two rent was paid on time. The rent for week three was not paid in week three, meaning that in week four your C-Corp paid "double rent" to leave a balance of zero. This is just an example; don't pay your rent late.

General Ledger of ABC Trading for the month of June 2022:

DATE	Details	Ref	Debit	Credit	Balance
1–7 June	Rent	JR-1	1000	1000	0
8–15 June	Rent	JR-2	1000	1000	0
16–22 June	Rent	JR-3	1000	0	1000
23–30 June	Rent	JR-4	1000	2000	0
Closing Bal					0

Financial Statements

Usually, financial statements are produced annually and reflect the profit or loss of your S-Corp. The concept is simple, assets-liabilities. There are some assets that do not seem like assets at first. The obvious ones are money in the bank, recorded as "cash," and the value of anything that your S-Corp owns, such as a company vehicle. Money owed to your S-Corp is an asset. Even though it isn't in your account yet, it will be when it becomes due (and paid). If you pay anything in advance, for instance, utilities, the amount is also an asset because, technically, it is still your money. Finally, your stockholding is an asset. It belongs to your S-Corp until it is sold.

Liabilities are made up of anything that your S-Corp owes or will owe, in the case of a 30-day account, for example. This includes monies owed but not yet due as repayments on a start-up loan or other type of finance.

If you are confused at this point, you need a bookkeeper. Don't worry if you are confused. You don't have any formal training in accounting, so actually, you should be confused.

Close out Your Financials

Back to the simple bit. At the end of the accounting period, you reconcile what you have recorded and start at zero for the upcoming accounting period.

Tax Time

When you are done with all of the above, you can file your return on Form 1120-S, available on the IRS website. Before we get there, it is necessary to lay out the why(s) and what(s) of S-Corps.

Employee Taxation

The reason for the development of S-Corps and pass-through taxation was to take tax pressure off smaller corporations, and the IRS has successfully done so. Employees have to be looked after in terms of medical care or unemployment, amongst other financial considerations, which means that S-Corps have to pay the following employee-related taxes.

Medicare and Social Security Taxes

The IRS requires S-Corps to withhold and pay Medicare and Social Security Taxes. Your S-Corp is also, as per IRS regulations, obliged to add their contribution to their employee tax. The percentage rate can vary from time to time, but you are looking at approximately 15.3% of each employee's wages.

Federal Unemployment Tax

The IRS requires S-Corps to pay this tax for permanent employees. It is a contingency for unexpected circumstances in which a worker finds themselves unemployed, so they can claim compensation. The rate is about 6% of each employee's wages.

Excess Net Passive Investment Tax

S-Corps were not intended as entities with large amounts of passive income, and as a result, S-Corps with significant passive income receipts are subject to corporation tax. The ruling is that an S-Corp that earns passive income is not responsible for tax on the first 25% of gross receipts, but any gross receipts that exceed the 25% mark do pay corporate tax on the percentage exceeded.

Shareholder Taxation

Federal Income Tax

S-Corp shareholders logically pay tax on their share of earnings accredited to the S-Corp. The tax rates fall within a large range, between 10% and 37%, even if the amounts due have not yet been distributed. It makes sense in that the money is essentially "owed" by the S-Corp to its shareholders.

Net Investment Income Tax

This form of tax applies to high-income earning shareholders who are not employees of the S-Corp. The high-income earning category is $200,000 per annum. If you are a couple that files your returns as such together, the threshold is $250,000 per annum. Remember that the tax applies to anything above the threshold and is set at exactly 3.8%.

State Income Tax

The rates differ from state to state, but they are relatively low, so no need to put a huge focus on this in terms of structure.

State Franchise Tax

Most states impose franchise tax requirements, and like State Income Tax, the rates vary, but there is an extra consideration for Franchise Tax, being the S-Corps annual income.

State Sales Tax

Like the above two categories, tax is most often payable on sales and/or income from services rendered, and the rates also vary from state to state.

Excise Tax

This tax is imposed on goods that are locally manufactured.

Unemployment and Workers Compensation Insurance

Most states require this of S-Corp shareholders for the same reason that non-shareholder employees benefit from Federal Unemployment Tax in adverse or unforeseen employment situations.

Tax Optimization

There are ways in which businesses can be structured in order to make them as tax effective as possible. At the end of the day, we all want to pay as little as possible… legally.

W-2 Income

If you have more than one shareholder, and one or more of your shareholders receive an employment income, otherwise known as W-2, you can structure the salaries on your S-Corp, so that shareholders with W-2 income are paid less. The salary still has to be reasonable for what that shareholder does, but having an employment income outside of the S-Corp means that such shareholders will dedicate less time to the S-Corp, thus justifying a smaller salary. The specific reason and saving come in due to the fact that smaller salaries can be kept below the social security tax threshold.

Husband and Wife High-Income Earners, Plus Children on the Payroll

This exercise keeps either the husband or the wife under the social security and Medicare tax thresholds. Let's say that they both earn $120,000; the entire $240,000 attracts social security and Medicare tax. If the wife was paid $200,000 and the husband $40,000, the husband's income is below the threshold, and the total tax saving is $8,750. You can also get your children to work after hours or during holidays as a way to even out family income to minimize tax.

Gifts

This one is not advisable, as it blurs the lines slightly, but if there is someone that your company is supporting, amounts can be paid and labeled as gifts to make income distribution look as if it falls under tax brackets. It is not illegal, but it borders on it, so if you choose to do this, please be very careful.

Form 1120-S

Now that you know the types of tax, we can get to the dreaded tax form, 1120-S. Depending on the size of your S-Corp, some sections of the form will be irrelevant. Like with anything, if you have never done it, then you will not know how to do it. For this part of the running of your S-Corp, you absolutely need a specialist. When your S-Corp is still growing, you probably want to hire a tax expert as and when needed, but this form you have to get correct. I will set out the basics below, split into sections. Note that the form does not refer specifically to parts, so I have divided the form into parts. Before I get there, I want to reiterate that you should not attempt this on your own unless you are formally trained or have experience in filing tax returns.

Part 1: Details

This part is easy; it requires all the information you already have at hand, like the name of S-Corp, EIN, address, date incorporated, number of shareholders, and other basic information.

Part 2: Income

I am not going to stipulate every single income line. The idea is to keep it simple and get the basics across.

This information is extracted from your accounting records and will look like this:

- Sales minus stock returns
- Cost of stock sold
- Gross profit/loss
- Net profit/loss
- Other income
- Total income

Part 3: Expenses

The same applies to focusing on the basics. This information also comes from your accounting records.

- Salaries
- Repairs to machinery
- Rent
- Interest
- Marketing
- Miscellaneous expenses
- Ordinary income/loss

Part 4: Tax and Payments

This is where complications come in, but the end result is your estimated tax, often referred to as a provisional tax. There are sections for passive income tax, as well as rebates, such as a returnable tax on fuel and tax penalties due to prior late filing. There is a section that requires an estimate of overpaid tax and an explanation of the calculations of each line item, depending on amounts and percentages.

Part 5: Other Information (Referred to as Schedule B on the Form)

This part starts with questions as to whether your S-Corp (other corporation) uses cash or accrual accounting, what the S-Corps primary business activity is, what the product is, and/or what service your S-Corp offers. It goes on to a list of questions about what I like to term "technicalities," such as whether a shareholder was classified as a disregarded entity. This is a complicated language for asking if your entity is registered for pass-through tax. The other questions mostly deal with turnover thresholds, percentage ownership, and information applicable to trusts or entities other than an S-Corp. When completing this section, you absolutely have to know exactly what you are doing.

Part 6: Shareholders Pro rata Share Items (Referred to as Schedule K on the Form)

This section deals with what one could call ancillary income. It requires the stipulation of real estate portfolios, rental income, capital gains, and losses. Furthermore, there is a component that focuses on things like biofuel tax and stipulations irrelevant to an S-Corp, like foreign taxes.

Part 6: Balance Sheets per Book (Referred to as Schedule L on the Form)

This part is assets and liabilities record. There are columns for asset values at the beginning and the end of the tax year, with areas to record depletable assets, shareholder loans, amortizable assets, and other categories whose names are hard to pronounce. Again, a large number of these sections are irrelevant to S-Corps.

Appoint an Expert

I am fully aware that I have been repeating this bit of advance, but I really do not want new business owners to attend to tax submissions on their own. I have stuck to the absolute basics, and from those, you can glean that the complicated parts have got to be addressed by an expert in the field.

Chapter Summary

Accounting/bookkeeping and tax returns are important from the point of view that if done correctly, the job of record-keeping becomes more effective. The term "collect and capture" describes the way in which you and your fellow shareholders and employees need to stay on top of the process. Every invoice, slip, check, and anything that forms proof of a transaction must be collected and captured into your accounting system AND must be filed physically.

The basis of accounting is maintaining a general ledger, the example of which is set out above. In addition, financial statements reflecting your S-Corps income or loss must be compiled and your financials closed out, from which point you can submit your tax returns.

Taxation is split into employee taxation and shareholder taxation, meaning non-shareholder employees, first off. Your S-Corp is subject to Medicare and Social Security Taxes, Federal Unemployment Tax, and Excess Net Passive Investment Tax. The latter is taxed highly as the S-Corp structure was not developed for largely passive income-earning businesses.

Shareholder taxation includes four types of state tax, i.e., Income, Franchise, Sales, and Excise Tax. The amounts differ from state to state, but in some states, not all four categories are taxed. The main taxation categories are Federal Income Tax and Net Investment Tax, which can be on the high side. Finally, the S-Corp is obliged to pay Unemployment and Workers Compensation Insurance, which caters to future situations of possible unemployment.

In terms of filing Form 1120-S, I broke up the sections, more for your information than the actual completion of the form. You want to get a tax expert, bookkeeper or accountant, or another expert to do this for you. If you attempt it yourself and make errors, you may cause your S-Corp to pay more tax than required. I would recommend sitting with your expert once he or she has completed the form, so they can explain it for your peace of mind.

CHAPTER 6

CLASSIFICATIONS, REGISTRATIONS, GOVERNMENT CONTRACTS, AND USEFUL TIPS

As you can imagine, the cross-section of businesses across the US is vast. For record keeping and data analysis, there has to be a way to accurately classify the type of business. I am not talking about S-Corp or C-Corp or LLC, but the actual industry in which your business operates. The U.S. Office of Management and Budget developed a coding system called the North American Industry Classification System (NAICS), which is used in business industry classification. It is not necessary to go into the breakdown of every classification, but basically, there are ten categories, within which there are more specific sub-categories. The said ten categories are as follows:

- Natural resources and mining
- Construction
- Manufacturing

- Trade, transportation, and utilities
- Information
- Financial activities
- Professional and business services
- Educational and health services
- Leisure and hospitality
- Other services (a type of miscellaneous category if your business does not fall into any of the other categories)

Your business chooses the most appropriate NAICS code for its industry classification, from the extended list. For example, Nursing falls under Educational and Health Services, which uses the code NAICS 623. Within the 623 categories are four sub-sectors identified as

- NAICS 623-1: Nursing Care Facilities
- NAICS 623-2: Residential Retardation, Mental Health, and Substance Abuse Facilities
- NAICS 623-3: Community Care Facilities for the Elderly
- NAICS 623-4: Other Residential Care Facilities

If you have a logistics S-Corp, the category will be Trade, Transportation, and Utilities. If your S-Corp is a catering business, it will fall under Leisure and Hospitality, and so on.

GSA Schedule

GSA is the acronym for General Services Administration, also called the Federal Supply Schedule (FSS), which works via the Multiple Award Schedule (MAS). The modus operandi is for the government to assist corporate companies with government supply contracts on a long-term basis. It is structured as one $45 billion dollar government contract across all industries and regulates pricing and terms of purchase. Basically, the government lays out the rules or qualifying standards, which does make the process more streamlined in a way that you know what to expect. The GSA Schedule is most often interested in contracts with corporations and federal agencies, but state and local governments can also become buyers.

GSA contracts are very valuable, whether your business is an S-Corp or otherwise, which means it is very important to know about how they work. One can look at it as an indefinite supply agreement, and the knowledge that your business is able to have an ongoing supply arrangement does give you peace of mind. The Office of Government Contracting and Business Development lists the following reasons, amongst others, for wanting to buy from smaller corporates:

- to ensure that large businesses do not outmuscle small businesses
- to gain access to the new ideas that small businesses provide
- to support small businesses as engines of economic development and job creation
- to offer opportunities to disadvantaged socio-economic groups

Specific Benefits of a GSA Schedule Contract

As above, the size of the contract means that there is a lot of supply. and service work that the government requires. The sales process is uniform, and it does assist in reducing competition from the point of view that you may have competitors that do not have contracts. Just a note, your business is not restricted to ONLY having government contracts.

What to Consider

If your business has supplied or provided services to the government in the past, getting a GSA contract will be very worthwhile, as be if your competitors have such contracts. Because there is uniformity and regulation to the process, work is fairly distributed. In terms of eligibility, your product or service must fit into one of the GSA Schedule categories, and your financials must reflect how your company is performing financially. You will have to show evidence that you have a history of providing services effectively if your business is service industry based. Product-based businesses must comply with the Trade Agreement Act, which requires that goods are manufactured in the US or a designated country, falling within the following categories:

- World Trade Organization Government Procurement Agreement Countries
- Free Trade Agreement Countries
- Least Developed Countries
- Caribbean Basin Countries

As you can imagine, the countries that fall within the above four groups are all on standard trading terms with the United States.

Does Your Business Have the Right Resources and Enough of the Right Resources?

You don't want to apply for a GSA contract if your business can't logistically or administratively handle the GSA contract or process. Do an assessment as to whether you have employees and/or employee shareholders that can handle what I will term the back-end or in-office requirements. Then make a call on whether there is enough time to get through the work required to obtain and successfully maintain the contract. You may have to employ someone, and the payoff for that would be getting more income-generating business, which justifies an extra salary. It has been estimated that it takes between six weeks and six months to obtain a contract, so it may be worth hiring a specialist on a freelance basis to take care of the process. Another reason to use a professional is that it is possible to secure 20-year term contracts, which will be a huge boost for any business whatsoever. Your business may be losing out on work by not having a GSA contract. So if you are in that situation and don't have the resources, you can start putting in place the things that will help you to get a GSA contract.

How to Sell to the Government

If your business has made a decision to get a GSA contract or look into the requirements in more detail, with a view to getting one, there is some background work needed. Committing to the process must be done comprehensively or not at all. My recommendation is to get on it, but here is what to do first.

Research

Firstly, you need to research the market. If your product or service is something that the government does not require or use, then you don't want to waste time going through the process. Fortunately, there is a lot of publicly accessible data on federal contracts. The top four resources to use are USASpending.gov, the Federal Procurement Data System, the Schedule Sales Query Plus, and the GSA eLibrary. You can find all four from a quick Google search. These are the kind of questions you should be looking to answer in this exercise:

- Who is your ideal buyer?
- What does your ideal buyer purchase (what product or service)?
- Who is your ideal buyer purchasing from?
- How does the procurement system work?

The first two are not difficult questions to answer, and prior to starting your business, you should have made comparisons with your competitors, so that information will be at hand. Thus the procurement system knowledge is mainly what you need to arm yourself with.

Registrations

You will have to register as a government contractor, even though you may already have your supply contract in place. If your business was to supply the government in any area, even without a GSA contract, this registration would be necessary. This is what it entails:

DUNS Number

Your business needs to be assigned a code that is then provided to the government in order for procurement-related matters. DUNS is a short form for Dun & Bradstreet Universal Numbering System, and a nine-digit number is an identification number unique to your business.

SAM Registration

The System for Award Management (SAM) is the portal under which several federal systems fall. The one relevant to being a government contractor is the Central Contractor Registration System.

Looking for Government Opportunities

SAM is continuously uploading information on available government work. If you go to SAM.gov, which you will be familiar with after your online registration, you will see several fields that allow you to search via code of industry. Set yourself up to receive email alerts, so you don't miss out on opportunities.

Another contract-finding resource open to GSA Schedule Contract holders is called eBuy. It is an RFQ, or Request for Quote online portal, and your searches will be via your unique codes.

If you have not gone through the registration process or are still busy with it, you could look to subcontract to businesses with existing government contracts. Subcontracting does not provide a direct opportunity, but keep in mind that the business that commissions you to subcontract could very possibly provide your S-Corp with regular work. Such an arrangement is great for learning from a business that is already established in the government sphere, but also for gaining credibility and growing your business. Large contractors with GSA contracts are encouraged to subcontract to smaller businesses as a "helping hand," to put it crudely. Essentially it is to give smaller businesses the ability to be successful, in a large business sphere, or at the least, competitive in that sphere.

DBA (Doing Business As)

This is not a requirement for your S-Corp, but if you are buying into a franchise, then you will probably need to apply for a DBA. Sole proprietorships and partnerships will most often use the term "doing business as," and it is actually legally required in certain states. Back to the franchise scenario, if you buy into a chain of restaurants as an S-

Corp, you obviously have to use the name of the franchise. Your S-Corp's legal name may be XYZ Corp, but it would then require a DBA, something like XYZ Corp, doing business as Kentucky Fried Chicken.

In the final part of this chapter, I am going to give you some practical business advice. Parts may seem obvious or just common sense, but these may be things that new business owners take for granted. I have come across people who observe the successes of experienced business owners, who have reached the point in their careers where they don't have to work hard and can enjoy the fruits of their labor. Just remember that these people put in the hard graft for many years to earn an earlier retirement and/or to take a backseat in the running of the business. If it is your goal to get to that point, it probably won't be easy, but remember that the work you put in now will pay off later.

Risks and Rewards

Some people are risk averse, and some get addicted to risk-taking. If you have started your own business, you are prepared to take a risk. When you have made that decision, you will note that other risks will materialize. Earlier I said that you need to be ready and not rush the launch of your business. It may be tempting to try and get your doors open as soon as possible because you want to start securing an income. If you are employed but intend to resign to set up your own business, do as much as you can while you are still getting an income, and only resign when you get to the point that you have to dedicate more time to the new business than you have available as a full-time employee. This tactic is certainly a mitigation of risk but is not the case in every situation.

The next set of risks will come when your business is operational, and you must consider what the worst possible outcome of a risk could be.

Let's say you are a clothing manufacturer, and you have a supplier that offers you a bulk discount if you order X amount of material. You require an increase in the amount of your business loan to make the payment to your supplier. There could be a few different worst cases, but let's say that the worst one is that you pay for the extra supply, get the discount, and make the clothing, but are unable to see half of it as demand is too low. As a result, you struggle to make repayments on the loan, and the discount is outweighed by the lack of turnover and the business loan interest.

In the best-case scenario, you increase the loan, buy the fabric, make the clothing, and sell it. You pay the extra portion of the loan back, and the discount has increased your profit margin significantly. The next step is to look at the practicality. If you have a customer that you can approach and ask if they will be prepared to take a bigger order, and you sign a contract to that effect, your risk has come right down. If that customer is unable to take a bigger order then that risk shoots up again. Yes, you may be able to find another customer that will take some of the extra clothing or even a new customer. However, you know for sure that if you don't buy more stock than usual, you will not have to increase your loan, and you will supply your customer/s as usual.

It all depends on your propensity to take risks. I am not saying do or do not take a risk, but make your decision based on as much information you can gather and the analysis of the possible risk.

Always Look for new Business

We all have some sort of network, and friends, family, and friends of friends or family could all be potential customers. Keep your eyes open and if there is an opportunity in a social setting, for example, then grab it if you can. Think about daily interactions with people and chances to hand out your business card (without being forceful). You may be thinking that business cards are old-fashioned, but they do work (Potters, 2022). Look for free opportunities to promote your business. There are many groups on social media or otherwise electronically, with the idea of promoting businesses and creating a community that supports each other's businesses. Google Ads are surprisingly cheap, attending conferences is sometimes free, and there is always the giant billboard option. Be as creative as you can!

Maintain Focus and Be Prepared to Put in the Hours

I hate to say it, but things will go wrong. No human in the history of time has gone through their whole life without anything going wrong. Business is the same, and you need to move on from disappointments by staying focused on your business goals. If you have that drive to succeed, which is evidenced in your focus you will be prepared to work overtime, on holidays, and over weekends. Your staff may not have the same drive, and you may have to pick up the ball where they drop it and fix things. As the adage goes, "you get out what you put in." If you know what you want to get out of your business, you will know what to put in. Always remember that!

Chapter Summary

Your S-Corp needs to be allocated an NAICS number, meaning that application must be made to the North American Industry Classification System for an identification number in terms of the classification of the industry that your business falls within. There are ten categories and in each category, there are sub-categories. For example, a catering business would fall under "Leisure and Hospitality."

Government contracts can be obtained via the GSA or General Services Administration, which has the goal of looking after smaller businesses and offering opportunities to socio-economically disadvantaged groups. The government, usually federal but also local, requires a lot of supply of resources, and performance of services, so getting government contracts can aid your business greatly.

The process is quite involved and requires research, so you need to make sure you or your staff can dedicate enough time to it. There are registrations on portals and allocations of specific numbers such as your DUNS number and SAM registration. All the information related thereto is contained in the above chapter. You may need to register a DBA (Doing Business As) if you are an S-Corp that has bought into a franchise.

You need to assess risk and paint the worst-case scenario and the best-case scenario. Assess the variables and what your business stands to gain. Perhaps you will find the risk too great to take, or you may find it an acceptable risk. If your business can handle the worst-case scenario, that is an indication that a potentially serious risk is mitigated, but if your business cannot handle the worst-case scenario, then the risk is not worth taking.

Every business wants more work, so you should be creative with marketing. So many opportunities to market your business in day-to-day life are present. Carry business cards, bring your business up in conversations, use social media, or Google Ads, and as I said earlier, perhaps try the billboard idea.

Maintaining focus is vital, especially when things go wrong, but if you really want your business to succeed, then you will maintain focus, and you will work hard and long to enjoy the rewards in the future.

CONCLUSION

I hope that you have enjoyed this book and have taken out of it what you expected to. You should, by this point, have established whether an S-Corporation will suit your particular business. If you are of the opinion that an S-Corporation is not the right vehicle for your business, then you should have an understanding of the other options open to you. The best way to conclude this book is to extract the main points, sequentially, so that you can be reminded of the nuts and bolts, and also so that you can refer back to the sections of interest.

An S-Corp is made up of shareholders and is limited to 100 individuals and one class of stock. Ownership is directly in line with percentage shareholding, and shareholders are taxed in their personal capacity. This is referred to as a pass-through tax, which means that there is no double taxation on the S-Corp and the shareholders. A major advantage is the limitation of liability, in that shareholders enjoy the protection of their personal assets.

Compared with Sole Proprietorships and Partnerships, an S-Corp is a better choice due to the limitation of liability. Sole Proprietorships treat the owner and the business as one, and Partnerships are also ordinarily subject to the limitation of liability. However, an LLP can be formed and is most useful in businesses that involve professionals, such as doctors or lawyers. LLP stands for Limited Liability Partnership, and the idea is that if one of the members is sued, the other members are not liable if the lawsuit is successful.

You then get non-profit entities that are most often part of social services, such as nursing, but for these purposes, they are not important. C-Corps differ from S-Corps in terms of shareholding and class of stock. The aforesaid is unlimited, and more than one class of stock is permissible. C-Corps are suited to large businesses that are seeking to further expand and look for international investors; they also provide the protection of limited liability. Limited Liability Companies or LLCs, also offer limited liability, of course, and have their tax advantages. Technically an S-Corp is not a business type but a tax classification, so an LLC can be an S-Corp if a decision is made to implement a tax election.

In deciding if an S-Corp is right for your business, it is necessary to consider salaries, which have an impact on taxation. Salaries must reflect the amount of work done and/or value to the business. You are paying yourself as a shareholder, which leaves open the possibility of paying yourself a small salary to avoid taxation. That method will not work as the IRS will look at your returns and reallocate monies that you have tried to distribute outside the realm of salaries.

There are factors to consider when deciding on salaries. I won't list them all, you can find them in chapter two, but a few examples are experience, duties, and responsibilities, in addition to time worked. The table with hypothetical comparisons between high, medium, and low salaries is a good marker to understand how it works practically. Generally, high salaries are subject to about a 2.9% tax saving, but if the determination of a reasonable salary comes in at under $132,900, the tax saving is much more significant. You can get a tax expert or accountant to assist you in making these determinations, as well as to give you general tax advice.

Because you are paying yourself and your fellow shareholders your salaries, a payroll system can be useful. You will pay a monthly fee to a payroll company, and for that fee, they will set up a deduction from the company cheque account into the individual shareholder's personal accounts. The same applies to non-shareholder employees.

Qualified Business Income (QBI) deduction is a tax break that was introduced in 2018, allowing a 20% deduction on your qualified business income, which is fairly significant. C-Corps do allow retirement plan contributions but are stringent in terms of amounts, and if you earn a salary from another source, tax rates on such sources are very high. You will have to do your sums to work out if you are scoring or losing on an overall basis.

There are seven steps to be followed when forming an S-Corp, I will list them below, but for the full breakdown, you will have to look at the beginning of chapter three:

☐ Decide on a name

☐ Check that the name is available

☐ Choose your state

☐ File and submit your articles of association (example template provided)

☐ Establish your board of directors

☐ Keep minutes of meetings

☐ Get your Employee Identification Number and make your tax status election

In terms of set-up, you can do a statutory conversion, also called a quick-status conversion, during which you file with the secretary of state. If you want to give your LLC S-Corp status, you will use a statutory merger, upon which the members will vote before filing. The least popular option is a non-statutory conversion, during which you will have to hire lawyers and accountants to create a corporation, transfer assets and liabilities, then liquidate and dissolve your LLC.

There are companies that will attend to the set-up for a fee, and they are listed under the particular section in chapter three.

Financing your business can be done via several methods. My recommended method is using a business lending marketplace, which is a one-stop shop when it comes to finding financing options. You only have to fill out one application form, which will then give you access to information on loans from a variety of lenders.

An operating agreement is not a stringent requirement, but it is wise to have one signed by all parties, and record the terms of the business relationship between the shareholders. See the example at the end of chapter three.

Mistakes in life are inevitable, and the same applies to business, but if you are aware of possible mistakes, you can avoid them or at least mitigate the backlash if they do happen. You can't be afraid of failure, you have made your decision, and you have to back yourself. Don't neglect to make a business plan, part of which will define your target market. It is also not advisable to do everything yourself. It is worth paying experts in order to save time and prevent future problems. You don't want to get the wrong investors or the wrong employees. So, do your due diligence in those regards. Understand what you need in terms of capital investment. My advice is to include a 20% contingency for unforeseen costs. Avoid wasting money, and not valuing your product correctly. You don't want to sell yourself short, but you also shouldn't be greedy. Don't get ahead of yourself by launching too early, trying to expand too quickly, and hiring too quickly. Lastly, do not make the mistake of neglecting to create a marketing plan. Here is a reminder of the components of a good plan:

- ☐ business mission
- ☐ key performance indicators
- ☐ your target market
- ☐ identify your competition
- ☐ your specific strategies and budget

Record keeping and accounting are two aspects that you need to stay on top of. It is best to update your books regularly and keep copies of absolutely anything that forms proof of transactions. When it comes to tax, remember that there are taxes such as Medicare and social security and federal unemployment tax that every S-Corp has to pay in relation to employees who are not also shareholders. You need to be aware of federal income tax and net investment as a shareholder, as well as certain state taxes and unemployment and worker's compensation insurance. All of these are explained in chapter four, as well as a breakdown of Form 1120-S, which your tax person will complete and submit on your behalf.

Your S-Corp will be classified with a unique code in line with whatever industry it falls under. The classifications were developed by the U.S. Office of Management and Budget and are controlled by the North American Industry Classification System (NAICS). This is required if your S-Corp wants to get government work. The way to do this is to apply for a General Services Administration Contract, which will allow your S-Corp to supply products or services to federal and sometimes state government departments. This thinking is that such contracts will help small to medium-sized entities compete with larger businesses and succeed in expanding, thus creating employment opportunities. In order to sell to the government, there are other admin registrations, for example, a DUNS number, which is an international allocation. Your S-Corp will also have to get registered on the System for Award Management, which is a portal for getting allocations of government work.

Lastly, three pieces of advice to remember in starting up and running a successful business. Analysis of risk and reward could make or break your S-Corp. Bad decisions have sent many businesses under. The simplest way of looking at it is in question form: Can my business cope if the risk does not pay off and the absolute worst result happens? If the answer is yes, then the risk may be justified. If the answer is no, then that risk is not worth taking (Potters, 2022). Always be on the lookout for new business, whether it be in social situations, at conferences, on social media, or any other form of advertising platform. You have got to maintain focus and be prepared to work hard. When things go wrong, and you need to fix them, you must call upon your focus when you have to work weekends and holidays. If you go in half-heartedly, then your success will be limited. So on top of choosing the right business entity, you have to make the choice to put in everything you have.

I would like to leave you with a quote that you can remember if things get tough or you encounter seemingly insurmountable problems. The quote is from Nelson Mandela, freedom fighter and Nobel peace prize winner:

"It always seems impossible until it's done."

GLOSSARY

Articles of Incorporation: Legal documents with your business details are to be filed with your state IRS office.

C-Corp: C-Corporation—Legally recognized types of corporation.

CCRS: Central Contractor Registration System—Where your business is registered as a government contractor.

DBA: Doing Business As—If the name of your business is different from the registered name, it is classified as DBA.

DUNS: Worldwide identification number for your business.

EIN: Employer Identification Number—Mandatory number identifying your business as an employer; received on application to the IRS.

Expenses: Total amount of money paid out for the year.

FSS: Federal Supply Schedule—GSA is also referred to as the FSS.

GSA: General Services Administration—Online system that controls government supply contracts given to businesses.

IRS: Internal Revenue Service—The government body responsible for taxation.

LLC: Limited Liability Company—Legally treated as a corporation or partnership.

LLP: Limited Liability Partnership—A partnership that is registered for limited liability. Usually a group of professionals, such as lawyers or doctors.

MAS: Multiple Award System—Interface on the GSA system.

NAICS Code: North American Industry Classification System Code— A unique code that identifies what economic sector a business fall into.

Payroll taxes: Tax on salaries.

Profit: Money received less money paid out (including salaries).

QBI: Qualified Business Income Deduction—Certain income is subject to tax deductions as per the IRS.

Revenue: Total amount of money received for the year.

RFQ: Request for Quotation.

SAM: System for Award Management—Portal for the awarding of government contracts.

S-Corp: S-Corporation—Legally recognized types of corporations.

Sole Proprietorship: An owner-run business.

ADDENDUM: CHECKLIST

The below checklist should be useful in consolidating the steps you need to take in order to get your S-Corp up and running. It doesn't only contain the admin parts, but some useful information in an ordered layout:

☐ Ascertain whether your business meets the qualifying requirements as discussed in chapter one.

☐ Consider whether you will benefit from the pass-through tax, taking into account the salaries that you intend to pay. Use the tables in chapter two, to provide assistance.

☐ Follow the seven-step process covered in chapter three, i.e.

    ☐ Decide on a name

    ☐ Check if the name is available

    ☐ Choose your preferred state

    ☐ File articles of association

    ☐ Appoint a board of directors

    ☐ Keep minutes of all meetings

    ☐ Apply for your businesses Employee Identification Number

- ☐ If you are converting an LLC, decide on statutory conversion, the merger of non-statutory conversion (not recommended due to complication and cost).
- ☐ Consider using a company that specializes in creating S-Corps. See the list of recommended companies in chapter three.
- ☐ Look at different financing options.
- ☐ Draw up an operating agreement, so that all parties involved know where they stand and what is expected of them.
- ☐ Things to avoid:
    - ☐ no business plan
    - ☐ disorganization
    - ☐ not defining your target market
    - ☐ not signing contracts
    - ☐ wasting money
    - ☐ incorrectly valuing your product or service
- ☐ Decide on your method of accounting (cash or accrual), and make sure you update your books regularly.
- ☐ Make sure you understand your tax requirements as set out in chapter five. Appointing a professional to assist in this department is highly recommended.
- ☐ Use chapter six to familiarize yourself with government contracts, the necessary registrations, and the requirements for becoming a government contractor.
- ☐ Work hard, put in the hours, and reap the rewards.

REFERENCES

§1.1244(c)–1 26 CFR Ch. I (4–1–20 Edition) - Govinfo.gov.
www.govinfo.gov/content/pkg/CFR-2020-title26-vol13/pdf/CFR-2020-title26-vol13-sec1-1244c-1.pdf.

Articles of incorporation. (2022, March 17). Legaltemplates.
https://legaltemplates.net/form/articles-of-incorporation/

Bajpai, P. (2022, July 16). *Understanding S Corporations.* Investopedia.
https://www.investopedia.com/articles/investing/091614/understanding-s-corporations.asp

Bryniarski, B (2020). *S Corporation Reasonable Compensation.* AICPA.
https://www.aicpa.org/resources/article/s-corporation-reasonable-compensation

Chi, C. (2022, December 8). *What is a Marketing Plan and How to Write One.*
Blog.hubspot. https://blog.hubspot.com/marketing/marketing-plan-examples

CT Corporation Staff. (2022, June 3). What are S-Corporations: Key Benefits and
More. Wolterskluwer. https://www.wolterskluwer.com/en/expert-insights/s-corporations#:~:text=Because%20of%20pass%2Dthrough%20taxation,(e.g.%2C%20the%20shareholders)

Glenn, D. (2022, May 9). *4 Things Doctors Should Consider Before Using an S-Corporation.* Taxcpafordoctors. https://www.taxcpafordoctors.com/4-things-doctors-should-consider-before-using-an-s-corporation/

GMP – Government Marketing & Procurement, L. (2021, July 15). *GSA schedules explained* - GMP - government marketing & procurement, LLC. https://www.gmpgov.com/gsa-schedules-explained/

Gonzalez, E. (2022, May 18). *Pros and Cons of S-Corps vs. C-Corps.* Fool. https://www.fool.com/the-ascent/small-business/document-management/articles/s-corp-vs-c-corp/

GSA. (2020, April 15). *TAA Designated Countries.* https://gsa.federalschedules.com/resources/taa-designated-countries/

Haskins, J. (2022, August 2). *Can I Change my LLC to an S-Corporation.* https://www.legalzoom.com/articles/can-i-change-my-llc-to-an-s-corporation#:~:text=to%20S%20corp.-,How%20to%20Change%20from%20LLC%20to%20S%20Corp.,an%20office r%20of%20the%20company.

Hurston, H. (2020, July 20). *S Corp Advantages and Disadvantages.* Wolterskluwer. https://www.wolterskluwer.com/en/expert-insights/s-corporation-advantages-and-disadvantages

Indeed Editorial Team. (2020, April 17). *6 Primary Types of Corporations and Their Differences.* Indeed. https://www.indeed.com/career-advice/career-development/types-of-corporations

Journals, B. (n.d.). *Should your startup become an S-Corp.* Brex. https://www.brex.com/journal/s-corp

Kappel, M. (2022, November 9). *How to Form a C-Corp.* Patriotsoftware. https://www.patriotsoftware.com/blog/accounting/form-c-corp/

Kopp, C. (2022, December 18). *Partnership: Definition, How It Works, Taxation, and Types.* Investopedia. https://www.investopedia.com/terms/p/partnership.asp#:~:text=A%20partn ership%20is%20an%20arrangement,form%20a%20limited%20liability%20p artnership.

Kopp, CM. (2022, June 15). *Partnership: Definition, How it Works, Taxation, and Types.* Investopedia. https://www.investopedia.com/terms/p/partnership.asp

Majaski, C. (2022, October 15). *LLC vs. S Corporation:* What's the Difference? Investopedia. https://www.investopedia.com/articles/personal-finance/011216/s-corp-vs-llc-which-should-i-choose.asp

Miller, MK. (2021, April 26). *5 Things You Should Know About Using a Lending Marketplace.* Lendio. https://www.lendio.com/blog/5-things-know-about-using-lending-marketplace/

Pash, A. (2022, February 26). *NAICS Codes: What Do They Mean For Your Business.* https://pricereporter.com/naics-codes-what-do-they-mean-for-your-business/?gclid=CjwKCAiA-dCcBhBQEiwAeWidtahUX_f8KduMRi_BivxmsYrjxd5YXjI5ExvWDgRULwGNnkopjGaZYBoCBwkQAvD_BwE

Pierce, M. (n.d.). *S Corp* - Single Class of Stock Rule. https://wyomingllcattorney.com/Incorporate-a-Wyoming-Corporation/S-Corp-Single-Stock-of-Class-Rule

Potters, C. (2022, July 3). *How to Grow a Successful Business.* Investopedia. https://www.investopedia.com/articles/pf/08/make-money-in-business.asp

Prakash, P. (2022, March 31). *DBA (Doing Business AS): What is it and How do I Register?* Nerdwallet. https://www.nerdwallet.com/article/small-business/dba-doing-business-as

Rosenberg, E. (n.d.). *How to Run Payroll for an S-Corp.* Collective. https://www.collective.com/blog/money-management/scorp-payroll/

S corp operating agreement: UPCOUNSEL 2023. (n.d.). https://www.upcounsel.com/s-corp-operating-agreement#:~:text=July%202%2C%202020%3A-,An%20S%20corp%20operating%20agreement%20is%20a%20business%20entity%20managing,of%20organizing%20the%20business%20operation.

Schooley, S. (2022, August 10). *20 Mistakes to Avoid When Starting a Business.* Businessnewsdaily. https://www.businessnewsdaily.com/7398-startup-mistakes-to-avoid.html

Treece, K. (2022, December 2). *Best Startup Business Loans of December 2022.* Forbes. https://www.forbes.com/advisor/business-loans/best-startup-business-loans/

Unknown. (2022, June 2). *Everything About S Corporation Formation in 2022.* https://www.offshorecompanycorp.com/insight/jurisdiction-update/everything-about-s-corp-formation-in-2022?gclid=Cj0KCQiAkMGcBhCSARIsAIW6d0CbjgvLkXZwtgtjd-FDe2xQVtN0VFuzZ5Ba2-JdCPt4_MyOBWV_OMgaAmRvEALw_wcB

Upcounsel. (2020, June 28). *Issuing Shares in an S-Corporation: What You Need to Know.* https://www.upcounsel.com/issuing-shares-in-an-s-corporation

Watkins, P. (2022, July 5). *Why Should You Convert Your LLC to an S-Corporation?* Novo. https://www.novo.co/blog/switch-from-llc-to-s-corporation

Woodman, C. (n.d.). *How to Keep Accounting Records for an S-Corporation.* Smallbusiness.chron. https://smallbusiness.chron.com/close-expense-account-57887.html

Made in United States
Orlando, FL
05 October 2023